Selina, Countess of

Selina, Countess of Huntingdon

Alan Harding

✛ EPWORTH

Copyright © Alan Harding 2007

The Author has asserted his right under the Copyright, Designs and Patents
Act, 1988, to be identified as the Author of this Work

British Library Cataloguing in Publication data

A catalogue record for this book is available
from the British Library

978 0 7162 0611 8

First published in 2007
by Epworth
4 John Wesley Road
Werrington
Peterborough PE4 6ZP

Typeset by Regent Typesetting, London
Printed and bound in Great Britain by
William Clowes Ltd, Beccles, Suffolk

Contents

Preface   ix

Abbreviations   xi

Acknowledgements   xiii

1 Religion in Eighteenth-Century England   1

2 The Evangelical Revival and the Origins of
   Methodism   16

3 Lady Huntingdon's Early Life and Marriage   25

4 Conversion   31

5 Widowhood and Its Aftermath   40

6 The 1750s: Lady Huntingdon's Circle Expands   50

7 The 1760s: Opening Chapels and Recruiting Helpers   65

8 The 1760s: Relations with Others in the Revival   81

9 Trevecca College   87

10 How the Connexion Spread and Operated   100

11 What It Was Like to Belong to a Countess of
    Huntingdon Congregation   115

12 Rows with Wesley   131

13 America: Bethesda Orphan House and Academy   147

14 Life at Trevecca College   164

15 Secession from the Church of England   171
16 Lady Huntingdon's Last Years   187

Bibliographical Note   206
Index   211

In memory of my parents

Henry James Harding (1901–1966)
Beatrice Dorothy Harding (1911–1972)

Preface

Very few men – and even fewer women – have the opportunity, or feel the need, to found a church of their own. Selina, Countess of Huntingdon, who is the subject of this book, is exceptional in doing just that. By the time she died, aged 83, in 1791, she had established a separate 'connexion' bearing her name, and consisting of more than sixty congregations. Her church had its own ordained ministry, its own ministerial training college, and its own statement of theological belief. In her lifetime, she had made a distinctive contribution to the eighteenth-century revival of evangelical religion in Britain, and her churches represented a small but important element in British nonconformity at the start of the nineteenth century. Even at the beginning of the twenty-first century there are still congregations in England bearing the name of the Countess of Huntingdon's Connexion.

None of this could have been predicted of the Earl's daughter who was born Selina Shirley in 1707. Nor indeed was it apparent, for a considerable period of her life, how significant she would later be. As we shall see, Selina was well into middle age before she embarked properly on the work for which she is remembered. The purpose of this book is to ask how it was that this woman became drawn into one of the major religious movements of her day, and how she moved from a supporting role to one of leadership on her own account. We shall examine the features of the church that she founded. (It quickly became known as her 'Connexion', and that is the term that we shall use throughout this book.) We shall look at some of the main events that happened to Lady Huntingdon and her Connexion, including her bitter quarrel with John Wesley, her experience as the absentee proprietor of an American slave plantation, and her reluctant decision to leave the Church of England. We shall end by asking about her legacy, and how worthwhile all this activity had been.

Why, though, should we bother to study her at all? Obviously the curiosity factor is a strong one. She led a remarkable life, and there was no-one quite like her, in the eighteenth century or since. We are used to aristocrats forming their own regiments or cricket teams, but an aristocrat who started her own *church* is in a class apart. More than that, her career sheds an important light on the social and religious life of the era in which she lived. She continually invites us to ask what it was about the eighteenth century that made it necessary or possible for someone like Lady Huntingdon to do what she did. She is also important in understanding the Evangelical Revival and the origins of Methodism. It is easy to think of the Evangelical Revival just in terms of John Wesley and of the evangelical party in the Church of England. Lady Huntingdon reminds us that there were other significant groups as well. In fact, her Connexion was (outside the Church) the largest of several English evangelical groups that differed from Wesley on theological grounds. She is key to appreciating the diversity of the Revival. Added to that, she knew virtually everyone who was anyone in the Evangelical Revival, so studying her takes us to the heart of the movement.

Before we begin to follow Lady Huntingdon's career, we shall consider what religious life was like in the England into which she was born. We shall also look at the nature of the Evangelical Revival, so that we can understand her place within it.

Abbreviations

Bridwell Library MS	Countess of Huntingdon correspondence in the Center for Methodist Studies, Bridwell Library, Perkins School of Theology, Southern Methodist University, Dallas
CF	The Cheshunt Foundation Archives, Westminster College, Cambridge
GRO	Archives of the Ebley Chapel of the Countess of Huntingdon's Connexion, deposited at the Gloucester Record Office
HMC	*Report on the Manuscripts of the late Reginald Rawdon Hastings Esq.* (London: Historical Manuscripts Commission, 1928–47)
Howell Harris's Visits to London	*Howell Harris's Visits to London*, ed. Tom Beynon (Aberystwyth: Cambrian News Press, 1960)
Huntington Library	Huntington Library, San Marino, California
JRL	John Rylands Library, Manchester
Life & Times of the Countess of Huntingdon	A. C. H. Seymour, *The Life and Times of Selina, Countess of Huntingdon*, 2 vols. (London, 1839)

LRO	Record Office for Leicestershire, Leicester and Rutland
Meth. Arch.	Methodist Connexional Archives in the John Rylands Library, Manchester
NLW	National Library of Wales, Aberystwyth
Nuttall, *Doddridge Calendar*	Geoffrey F. Nuttall, *Calendar of the Correspondence of Philip Doddridge DD (1702–1751)* (London: Historical Manuscripts Commission, 1979)
Roberts, *Selected Trevecka Letters*	*Selected Trevecka Letters, 1742–1747 & 1747–1794*, ed. G. M. Roberts (Caernarvon: Calvanistic Methodist Bookroom, 1956 & 1962)
Trevecka Letters	Trevecka Letters Collection, National Library of Wales, Aberystwyth
Wesley, *Journal*	*The Journal of the Rev. John Wesley, A.M.*, ed. N. Curnock, Standard Edition (London, 1938)
Wesley, *Letters*	*The Letters of the Rev. John Wesley, A.M.*, ed. J. Telford, Standard Edition (London, 1931)
Wesley, *Works*	*The Bicentennial Edition of the Works of John Wesley*, vols. xx–xxiii, ed. W. R. Ward and R. P. Heitzenrater (Nashville: Abingdon Press, 1991–95)

Acknowledgements

Quotations from original documents are reproduced by courtesy of:

The Bedfordshire and Luton Archives and Records Service

The Cheshunt Foundation Archives, Westminster College, Cambridge

The Trustees of the Congregational Memorial Hall Trust

The Ebley Chapel of the Countess of Huntingdon's Connexion

The Huntington Library, San Marino, California

The Record Office for Leicestershire, Leicester & Rutland

The Archives and History Committee of the Methodist Church

The University Librarian and Director, the John Rylands Library, The University of Manchester

The Manuscript Collection, Bridwell Library, Perkins School of Theology, Southern Methodist University, Dallas, Texas

The National Library of Wales, Aberystwyth

(*The spelling and punctuation of the quotations used in this book have been modernized for ease of understanding. For the same reason, abbreviated words have generally been given in full. In line with general usage, the spelling 'Trevecka' has been used throughout, except in the case of Lady Huntingdon's College, which was normally written 'Trevecca'.*)

1

Religion in Eighteenth-Century England

⌐⌐⌐

The eighteenth century followed nearly 200 years of dramatic change in religious and political life in England – just as it did in many other parts of Europe. For the ordinary worshipper under the Tudors, the changes that affected parish life (whether welcome or not) must often have been bewildering. Under Henry VIII and Edward VI, the rich pattern of processions, commemorations, and Latin masses of the late medieval church were replaced with increasing speed by the beliefs and practices of continental Protestantism. Mary Tudor's brief reign put that whole process into reverse, before Elizabeth sought to fix the Church of England at some middle point between the old religion and the new.

The Elizabethan compromise meant that many advocates of reformed beliefs and practices – Presbyterians, Baptists and others – were left dissatisfied by the form the Established Church had taken. Their main objection was to the fact that it still had bishops and still used set prayers. Many of the religious controversies of the seventeenth century were concerned with the desire of such people either to turn the Church of England itself into the sort of church they favoured, or else to pursue their own vision of Christianity in separate congregations outside the national church. The former approach triumphed temporarily during the Cromwellian period. But the restoration of Charles II showed that

1

these more radical Protestants had no permanent home within the Church of England. For 25 years they were persecuted. Then (after the accession of William and Mary, following the Glorious Revolution of 1688) they were tolerated as separate denominations. But the dawn of the eighteenth century saw them formally outside the mainstream of English civic and religious life

This marginalization of the groups known collectively as 'Dissenters' had a dramatic effect upon their size and social mix. Many of their more economically and socially powerful adherents were absorbed back into the Church of England. And their overall numbers shrank significantly. Around 1700 they had about 30,000 adherents; by 1740 that number had halved. Decline continued through the middle years of the eighteenth century, until Dissent was revitalized by the Evangelical Revival in the final decades. The Dissenters, in this demoralized state, provide an important backdrop to the emergence of Lady Huntingdon's Connexion.

For Roman Catholics in eighteenth-century England, the legal position was rather different. For much of the century it was technically illegal for them to hold services, although in many parts of the country they were able to do so with only occasional interruptions. Like the Dissenters, however, Catholics were an endangered minority. As with the Dissenters, some of the wealthier Catholic families were drawn to join the Established Church and mainstream society – with damaging effects on any Catholic congregations dependent upon them. By 1740 the Catholic community in England was half the size it had been 50 years earlier. It continued in a weakened state until émigrés and immigration gave it new life at the end of the century. Roman Catholics do not figure very much in the story of Lady Huntingdon. But they were a continuing source of anxiety to many Protestants, who saw them as a threat to all that they thought the Reformation had achieved. (At the height of Lady Huntingdon's doctrinal dispute with John Wesley, one of the worst insults that her followers produced was that Wesley's principles were 'too rotten even for a Papist to rest upon'!)

The vulnerable condition of both Protestant Dissenters and Catholics in the early eighteenth century emphasized the dominant position of the Church of England. The Church was still the main focus of the nation's religious life. But although it appeared to have triumphed after the conflicts of the sixteenth and seventeenth centuries, there were also respects in which it had suffered. For one thing, the Reformation had weakened the Church financially, leaving some parishes with insufficient income to maintain a pattern of worship. The Reformation had also greatly increased lay influence and control. Then in the seventeenth century the Church of England lost some of the rich diversity that it had originally enjoyed. In the Cromwellian period its sacramental traditions were undermined. In 1662, after the restoration of Charles II, it lost many of its more Protestant ministers, when they were ejected from their livings and left the Church. Then, after the accession of William and Mary in 1688, a significant group of High Church clergy (the so-called 'non-jurors') left the Church rather than break their oath to the deposed King James II.

Perhaps most importantly of all, the Church of England was no longer the *only* lawful religion that people could follow. The Toleration Act of 1689 meant that freedom of choice in religion was now recognized by law, so that the Established Church was on the way to becoming just one denomination among several. People could now choose which church to go to, and (increasingly) whether to go to church at all. Although the Anglican Church was still legally the established religion of the nation, in practice it was competing in a market place – and competing not only with other denominations, but also with religious indifference. Over the eighteenth century the numbers attending Anglican services declined relative to the population at large. The trouble was that the Church's apparently dominant position obscured the need for it to do more to sell itself. Nor did it have an effective mechanism for responding to new challenges like the Industrial Revolution, or for tackling some of its inherited organizational problems, especially the unequal spread of church wealth. It was this inequality that contributed to some of the main perceived abuses of the eighteenth-century Church of England.

The popular view of eighteenth-century clergy has long been that they were lax and worldly, and that they neglected their parishioners' spiritual needs. Recent scholarship has modified that view to some extent, finding signs of committed Christian activity among both clergy and lay people, in various parts of the country. We shall consider some instances of this in a moment. There is certainly no avoiding the fact that many churchmen thought of ecclesiastical appointments in terms of property and income. The principal evidence for this is the practice of pluralism (vicars or rectors holding more than one 'living') and non-residence (not living in their parishes). Obviously there is a link between these factors, since a priest responsible for more than one parish cannot live in each of them.

Non-residence certainly seems to have increased during the eighteenth century: by the early nineteenth century some 60 per cent of parishes had no resident vicar or rector. Pluralism seems also to have got worse during the century, and attempts to restrict it were not helped by the fact that even some bishops augmented their income by holding wealthy livings in addition to their sees. A good example of this was Robert Drummond, a future Archbishop of York, and by the standards of his age a faithful church leader, who held the living of Bothall in Northumberland throughout the 13 years he was Bishop of St Asaph. Although it seems that Drummond never lived at Bothall, the parish was not neglected, since he paid curates to serve in his place. But the sums involved reveal a key point about the eighteenth-century Church – the fact that there was an underclass of poor curates, available to serve parishes on behalf of their more fortunate brethren. Drummond's tenure of Bothall increased his income by £280 a year. But out of this he paid his curates, in line with normal rates, just £34.10s.

It is the meagre amount on which curates were expected to survive that weakens the argument that pluralism was necessary because of the poverty of some parishes. Certainly the value of livings varied considerably: from over £1,000 a year in a few cases, down to under £100. Even so, very few vicars would have been as poor as curates were routinely expected to be. And the supply of curates does not appear to have kept pace with the demands for their services: for example, an inquiry in 1812 found that there were 4,813 non-resident incumbents, but only 3,694 curates available to supply for them. Thus there were instances of complete neglect – as the evangelical philanthropist Hannah More had discovered in the West Country, late in the eighteenth century:

> I asked the farmers if they had no resident curate; they told me they had a right to insist on one; which right, they confessed, they had never ventured to exercise, for fear their *tithes should be raised* . . .
>
> . . . It is grievous to reflect that while we are sending missionaries to our distant colonies, our own villages are perishing for lack of instruction. We have in this neighbourhood thirteen adjoining parishes without so much as a resident curate.

> Quoted in Annette M. B. Meakin, *Hannah More*, 1911, pp. 293–4.

Despite these very obvious weaknesses in the eighteenth-century Church (and the dire situation in some areas, like that encountered by Hannah More) a regular round of worship and ministry seems generally to have been maintained. Probably most parishes had a service each Sunday, and some, particularly in urban areas, managed two. Communion services, which can be regarded as some sort of indicator of spiritual commitment, were not as rare a phenomenon as was once thought. Although quarterly Communions were the norm in many areas, it is clear that more frequent celebrations were sometimes to be found, even in quite small centres of population.

There were other signs of Anglicans taking their religion seriously and seeking to promote it. One example occurred in the very last year of the seventeenth century when a society was established, aimed at improving the education of clergy and laity, including children. One of its founding documents stated:

> Whereas the growth of vice and immorality is greatly owing to the gross ignorance of the principles of the Christian religion, we ... do agree to meet together, as often as we can conveniently, to consult (under the conduct of the Divine Providence and assistance) how we may be able by due and lawful methods to promote Christian Knowledge.
>
> Quoted in W. K. Lowther Clarke, *A History of the SPCK*, 1959, p. 13.

The name they chose was the 'Society for Promoting Christian Knowledge' (SPCK). Among its original activities were the establishment of charity schools and the provision of Bibles and other religious literature. The society contributed to the extensive sales of popular Christian literature that occurred during the eighteenth century – itself an indication of the desire that many people felt to develop their religious understanding and devotional lives. SPCK was concerned with work abroad, as well as in Britain, and in 1701 a separate body was formed to take forward its missionary purposes in the American colonies and the West Indies, the 'Society for the Propagation of the Gospel' (SPG). Interestingly, in view of what we have been discussing above, the prime mover behind both societies, the Revd Thomas Bray, left his Birmingham parish in the care of a curate for many years, so that he could go to London and then America to promote his missionary interests. (In a similar way, as we shall see, the beneficed clergy who served Lady Huntingdon generally left their parishes in the care of curates.)

These two national societies were part of a broader pattern of individuals joining together for spiritual or philanthropic purposes. Another instance of this was the so-called 'religious societies', which first appeared in London in the late seventeenth century, and then spread more widely around the country. These were groups of religiously minded lay people, generally under the leadership of the clergy, who committed themselves to a discipline of daily prayer and regular meeting. Such groups are to be found for several decades of the early eighteenth century. They may have declined after this, though there is evidence that some societies were still active in the 1730s – thus overlapping with the beginnings of the Evangelical Revival. Certainly the underlying principles of the religious societies made an important reappearance during the Revival – for example, in the band and class meetings of Wesleyan Methodism and in the 'societies' that, as we shall see, were a feature of many congregations in the Countess of Huntingdon's Connexion.

Humanitarian schemes were also important in the eighteenth century, whether or not directly prompted by religious beliefs. During the century, there were initiatives to found hospitals, to reform the prisons, and (eventually) to abolish slavery. An outstanding example of an eighteenth-century philanthropist was the retired sea captain Thomas Coram, whose heart was moved by the sight of abandoned infants, left to die on the streets of the capital. Coram badgered some of the most eminent people of his day – in the aristocracy, in the arts, in music and in medicine – into supporting his efforts to tackle this evil, efforts which led to the establishment of the Foundling Hospital in London in 1741.

What do we know of the commitment of eighteenth-century clergy? A detailed insight into the life of one beneficed clergyman is to be found in the diaries of James Woodforde, rector of a Norfolk country parish during the last quarter of the century. They give a mixed picture. Woodforde clearly aspired to the lifestyle of a country gentleman; he makes a great deal of his contacts with the squire of the parish, and he tells us much more about what he had for dinner than what he believed or preached. But he resided in his parish (apart from holidays spent with his relatives in Somerset) and during most of his tenure he undertook the church duties himself. He was familiar with the poor of the parish, as well as with the rich; he frequently gave money or food to the sick and needy; and he would hand back the church fees due to him when he judged the person concerned was hard up. And notice this diary entry after the burial of a young man in the parish:

> Harry Nobbes was only 25 years old . . . His poor aged mother attended at the funeral and came to see me after with tears in her eyes to thank me for what I had done for him. But O Lord! Not unto me but unto thy divine goodness be ascribed all the praise.
>
> James Woodforde, *Diary* for 9 December 1790, Oxford: Oxford University Press, 1978, p. 389.

This is hardly the stereotyped picture of an absent or indifferent eighteenth-century parson.

In the nature of things, not many of the poorer, unbeneficed, clergy left much historical evidence of their work. But Professor Gordon Rupp uncovered one who, if not representative of all his brethren, showed what an eighteenth-century curate could be capable of:

> John Bold [was] curate of Stoney Stanton in Leicestershire, where he lived faithfully and devotedly for nearly fifty years, living contentedly on one meal a day in one hired room in a farm, before whose thronged and open hearth he did his reading. He was also a devoted catechist, from whose parish crime seems to have disappeared. All this on £30 a year, and heaven too.
>
> E. G. Rupp, *Religion in England, 1688–1791*, Oxford: Clarendon Press, 1986, p. 496.

Lay people could also show signs of deep personal devotion. A good example was Dr Johnson, whose spiritual wrestling, as revealed in his diaries and prayers, shows a man who took the implications of his religion extremely seriously. Johnson usually took Communion only once a year, but he preceded it each time with intense self-examination and the composition of a prayer for the occasion. The one he wrote before what he expected would be his last Communion gives a moving insight into an eighteenth-century Anglican at prayer:

> Almighty and most merciful God, I am now, as to human eyes, it seems, about to commemorate for the last time, the death of thy Son Jesus Christ, our Saviour and Redeemer. Grant, O Lord, that my whole hope and confidence may be in his merits, and thy mercy; enforce and accept my imperfect repentance; make this commemoration available to the confirmation of my faith, the establishment of my hope, and the enlargement of my charity; and make the death of thy Son Jesus Christ effectual to my redemption . . . Support me, by thy Holy Spirit, in the days of weakness, and at the hour of death; and receive me, at my death, to everlasting happiness, for the sake of Jesus Christ. Amen.

> Quoted in James Boswell, *Life of Johnson*, Oxford Standard Authors, 1953 edition, pp. 1391–2.

These were some of the external expressions of religious faith during the eighteenth century. But what of the substance of that faith?

We have, of course, to be cautious in generalizing about the beliefs of eighteenth-century Christians, just as we would about Christians in our own day. That said, there are certain broad themes that stand out. One of these was the intellectual climate of the time. The scientific developments of the seventeenth century – developments that we associate with thinkers like Isaac Newton

– were not anti-religious in origin. To a large extent, indeed, scientific progress was made possible by the belief that God had created the world according to clear principles – principles that were waiting to be discovered by the application of scientific methods. Science was thus about understanding the works of God. And the more science went on, the more the initial hypothesis appeared to be borne out: the universe did indeed conform to rational rules. Those rules were themselves evidence of the wisdom and majesty of God. So some people came to think of God like a master technician, some sort of celestial watchmaker, who had set the universe effortlessly ticking away for all eternity. The trouble about that model, however, was that it removed any need for God to remain involved with his creation. A perfect creation will not go wrong, so there is no need for its creator to intervene to put it right.

This train of thought led some people to what is called 'deism' – the belief that although God created the world, he plays no further part in it. Such a system, of course, runs directly counter to the Christian faith. It leaves no room for revelation, no room for Christ, and no need for any sort of church. Anything we know of God, said the deists, is to be found through the natural order. It followed for them that Jesus must have been either deceived or a deceiver. A flavour of the deist challenge to orthodox Christianity is to be found in the writings of Thomas Woolston, who claimed in his *Six Discourses on the Miracles of Our Saviour* (1727–1729) that any reasonable reading of the Gospels showed Jesus to have been 'a juggling impostor [and] a strolling fortune-teller'.

Deism was most at its height in the early decades of the eighteenth century. But though it declined in intellectual popularity thereafter, it marked an important watershed in English religious life. Never before had the basic tenets of Christianity been questioned so extensively or so publicly. And it left its mark in continued critical scrutiny of the Bible, particularly those parts of the New Testament that were of most significance for belief in the divinity of Jesus and the doctrine of the Trinity. This was as much an issue for those inside the Church as for those outside. In 1712, for example, the Revd Samuel Clarke, rector of the fashionable London church of St James, Piccadilly, had caused controversy with *The Scripture Doctrine of the Trinity*, in which he analysed over a thousand biblical texts to support his argument that God the Father was supreme over the other Persons of the Trinity. He produced a revised Anglican liturgy that reflected his theological conclusions. The Trinity is one of those tenets of the Christian faith which the Early Church developed out of its reflection on the redemption won by Christ – but it is a belief for which there are only limited biblical foundations. As the liberal Bishop Richard Watson put it, later in the century:

> We do not object to the doctrine of the Trinity because it is above our reason, and we cannot apprehend it; but we object to it because we cannot find that it is either literally contained in any passage of Holy Writ, or can by sound criticism be deduced from it.
>
> Quoted in R. N. Stromberg, *Religious Liberalism in Eighteenth Century England*, 1954, p. 41.

These issues came into public prominence again in the 1770s, when the so-called Feathers Tavern Petition sought to persuade Parliament to release Anglican clergy from having to subscribe to the Thirty-nine Articles, which include belief in the Trinity. The Petition failed, and some of its supporters left the Church of England, including the Revd Theophilus Lindsey (as it happened, a family friend of Lady Huntingdon) who went on to found a Unitarian chapel in London.

These theological speculations were not confined to the Established Church. There are also cases of Dissenters abandoning the belief that Jesus had equal standing with the Father, or even that he possessed divine status at all. This might happen to whole congregations, or to sections within a congregation, in which case splits might well occur. Sometimes it was congregations who remained orthodox, while their ministers flirted with more radical ideas. In 1733, one Suffolk congregation regretted that:

> The faithful labourers in Christ's vineyard are so few, and the deceitful and sophisticated corruptors of the word and doctrine so many, that it appears exceedingly difficult for a church really adhering to good old Protestant doctrines to be again settled with a suitable and agreeable Pastor.
>
> Quoted in Doreen Rosman, *The Evolution of the English Churches, 1500–2000*, Cambridge: Cambridge University Press, 2003, p. 129.

The same lament might have been heard at many points in the eighteenth century. As we shall see, the fact that there were orthodox Dissenters around, anxious for what they regarded as sound teaching and preaching, was to be an important contributory factor in the spread of groups like Lady Huntingdon's Connexion.

The majority of eighteenth-century Christians were probably untouched by these profound doctrinal issues. Few, however, would have been unaffected by the prevailing theological approach of the times, an approach now often known as 'latitudinarianism'. Latitudinarianism resulted in part from the liberalism that we have just described, and in part also from unpleasant memories of the intense religious controversies that had plagued the previous centuries – to which most people were anxious not to return. Latitudinarianism was an imprecise term, which could cover a range of beliefs and positions. But at its heart it saw God as a kindly creator, one who wanted the best for his creatures, and who did not place heavy expectations upon them. Revealingly, a text much favoured by eighteenth-century preachers was: 'His commandments are not grievous.' Latitudinarians thought that biblical passages about Christians facing hardship and persecution applied only to the early centuries of the Church – and not to the enlightened, tolerant world of the eighteenth century. They held a faith that was moderate, rational and ethical, and one which avoided the more mystical and mysterious aspects of religion. They wanted to rid it of what they saw as the remains of medieval superstition. (That did not mean, of course, that eighteenth-century men and women were not interested in the Middle Ages: paradoxically, 'gothic' novels and ruins became increasingly popular as the century went on.)

This rather easy-going approach to religion was probably held by the majority of eighteenth-century religious leaders in England. It is an attitude that should not be dismissed lightly. There is much to admire about a church that is reluctant to place heavy moral or religious burdens on people. Too often through history churches have done precisely the opposite. Latitudinarianism was an important part of the contemporary religious scene, and the Evangelical Revival was a reaction against it.

There is one other theme in eighteenth-century religion that we should notice. It too is important in understanding the evangelicals, because, in a sense, they were a reaction against it as well. This is what might be called the High Church tradition in Anglicanism, although the term did not mean 'high church' in quite the sense used today. The people we are talking about were the spiritual heirs of the Anglican giants of the early seventeenth century – of priest-poets like John Donne and George Herbert, or saintly bishops like Lancelot Andrewes and John Cosin. Their objective was the disciplined pursuit of holiness and dedication to God, and it was this tradition that fostered the religious societies that we have already noticed. But although the poetry of Donne and Herbert vibrates with joyful love for God, the tradition had become more austere as the seventeenth century went on. The titles of two works written in the middle of the century give an indication of the tone of High Church piety: *The Rule and Exercise of Holy Living* (and its sequel *Holy Dying*) by the future bishop Jeremy Taylor, and the anonymous *The Whole Duty of Man*. To these indicative titles may be added a third, written in the 1720s, *A Serious Call to a Devout and Holy Life* by William Law. His message was that life was to be taken desperately seriously, filled with good works, with no room for pleasure or relaxation, and with regular self-examination and resolutions to do better. Some of his chapter headings give the flavour of his approach:

'Of the great danger and folly, of not intending to be as eminent and exemplary as we can, in the practice of all Christian virtues'

'We can please God in no state, or employment of life, but by intending and devoting it all to his honour and glory'

'That not only a life of vanity, or sensuality, but even the most regular kind of life, that is not governed by great devotion, sufficiently shows its miseries, its wants and emptiness, to the eyes of the world.'

William Law, *A Serious Call to a Devout and Holy Life*, chapters 3, 4 and 13.

It is an admirable creed, and in many ways just how Christians should live their lives. But it was not a joyful faith, and it risked missing out on the freedom and fullness of life which are an equally important part of the Christian gospel. The evangelical message (at least in some of its forms) offered an escape from this austerity. This is why it appealed strongly to a number of dedicated Christians who had been brought up in the traditions of High Church piety. (Interestingly, Law himself was to move on from his earlier rigorous view of the disciplined Christian life, to a more mystical phase that emphasized prayer and the work of the Holy Spirit.)

These are some of the features of religious life in eighteenth-century England. In the next chapter we shall look at the origins of the Evangelical Revival, and consider how it fits into this broader religious context.

2

The Evangelical Revival and the Origins of Methodism

⸙

What do we mean by the Evangelical Revival? What was being 'revived'? If those involved had been asked this question, they might have answered in terms partly of beliefs, and partly of attitudes. So far as beliefs were concerned, they would have said that they were bringing back to prominence the doctrines that had been at the heart of the Reformation. They would have stressed particularly the belief that mankind was innately sinful and under the fully deserved judgement of God; that salvation was only possible through Jesus Christ; and that such salvation was a free gift from God, rather than something that had to be earned by good works. For Anglican evangelicals, these beliefs were enshrined within the key texts of their church – particularly its doctrinal statement, the Thirty-nine Articles, and the services of the *Book of Common Prayer*. This was something they often stressed, when they were accused by other Anglicans of introducing new ideas or novel doctrines.

> Man is very far gone from original righteousness, and is of his own nature inclined to evil, so that ... [he] deserveth God's wrath and damnation ...

> We are accounted righteous before God, only for the merit of our Lord and Saviour Jesus Christ by Faith, and not for our own works or deserving ...

Works done before the grace of Christ are not pleasant to
God . . .

Book of Common Prayer of the Church of England, Articles IX, XI and
XIII.

For many of those who became involved in the Revival, the step
of affirming these doctrines represented a dramatic turnaround,
rather than the result of a process of intellectual reflection. They
would be gripped by these beliefs in a highly personal way, and
very often at a point of crisis – they would perhaps have been
agonizing over their own sinfulness for some time, before they
were suddenly able to find peace and reassurance through commitment to Christ. They would then be amazed that God's grace
extended even to *them*. Revealingly, a term they sometimes used
to describe the experience was being 'savingly converted', and
they were not afraid of mixing their religion with emotion and
strong feelings.

The evangelicals' conviction that human beings were in great
danger – danger from which only faith in Christ could rescue
them – gave an urgency to their preaching, and a seriousness
to their lives. They rejected the latitudinarians' belief that in a
rational world everything would be all right; it would *not* be all
right without a radical change of direction. Seriousness about
religion was key. They preached, as one of them said, 'as a dying
man to dying men'. And such was the immediacy of the need that
the niceties of church practices – especially parish boundaries
– could not be allowed to get in the way of the message.

What did evangelicals hope to achieve? The answer changed
as the century went on, and also differed between the various
groups within the Revival that we shall shortly be examining. At
the start, most would have said that they wanted to re-establish
their key doctrines as the core beliefs of the churches to which
they belonged – in the Church of England, or within the various
sections of Dissent. Only as time went on were they forced to

lower their sights, and accept that they were not going to win over all their co-religionists. When that happened, they had to be content either to be just a party within their own church, or to break away into separate sects on the outside. With their theological aims went social ones, to bring society back from the moral decay into which they believed it had fallen. They were careful not to imply that moral behaviour would lead to salvation. But a society that was 'godly, righteous, and sober' (in the words of the *Book of Common Prayer*) was what most of them wanted.

Although the Evangelical Revival was most immediately a reaction to some of those features of contemporary religious life that we considered in the previous chapter – the easy-going attitude of the latitudinarians, the lack of emphasis on Reformation doctrines, and the austerity of the High Churchmen – it was also part of a more general phenomenon. Other parts of the British Isles, Europe and North America experienced similar revivals in the early eighteenth century. The leaders in the various countries regarded themselves as part of that wider movement, and there was a regular exchange of information between them. One of the most significant of the overseas groups, so far as the revival in England was concerned, was the Moravian Brethren. The Brethren were a Protestant group, originally from Bohemia and Poland, which had settled at Herrnhut in Saxony in the 1720s under the protection and leadership of another aristocratic religious leader, Count Nicholas Zinzendorf. Thereafter they undertook missionary activity in various countries, including establishing a society in London from 1738, and subsequently in other parts of England. It is an interesting comment on English church life at the time that the country was regarded as part of the mission field. Although there were later to be disputes between the Moravians and groups within the British Revival, the Brethren's piety and dedicated lives had a major impact on John Wesley in the lead-up to his conversion:

I began to learn German, in order to converse a little with the Moravians, six-and-twenty of whom we have on board, men who have left all for their Master, and who have indeed learned of Him, being meek and lowly, dead to the world, full of faith and of the Holy Ghost.

John Wesley, on board ship for America; *Journal* for 17 October 1735.

As we shall see, Lady Huntingdon also had contacts with the Moravians, at a key stage in her own religious development.

Within England and Wales, the Evangelical Revival was not a single movement, but was made up of a number of separate strands, even though there were often links between them. Outsiders were sometimes puzzled by these different elements, and failed to distinguish between them: to many observers they were all just 'Methodists'. Nevertheless, it is instructive to look briefly at these various elements, in order to understand the context in which Lady Huntingdon operated. Her connexion is best understood as one among a number of separate organizations that operated under the broad umbrella of the Evangelical Revival.

One of the first signs of revival can be detected very early in the century, when a South Wales rector, Griffith Jones, began itinerant (that is, travelling) preaching and started a system of circulating charity schools. His influence led, in the 1730s, to the conversion of two other clergymen, Daniel Rowlands and Howel Davies. These two were joined by the layman Howel Harris, and the three became a major force behind a revival movement that crossed Wales. So successful was this that by 1750 there were over 400 local societies, grouped together in districts, under the over-all direction of a body known as the Welsh Association. They are especially interesting as a revival movement that significantly predated Wesleyan Methodism. In fact, the Wesleyans played only a limited role in Wales during the eighteenth century, unlike Lady Huntingdon who actually located her college there. Some of the Welsh leaders, particularly Howel Harris, were to take an important part in the Revival in England.

It is in the late 1720s that the story of John and Charles Wesley first becomes significant, because of the group of pious young men that formed around them in Oxford – the so-called 'Holy Club'. The Club members committed themselves to a strict regime of good works and spiritual self-improvement, and they attended Holy Communion regularly. In other words, they displayed some of the High Church piety that was a distinguishing feature of the religious societies we looked at earlier. The Holy Club was to spawn three distinct groups within the coming revival in England. The first of these, chronologically, derived from the activities of a latecomer to the Club, George Whitefield. Whitefield's conversion experience occurred in 1735, while he was still in his very early twenties. After ordination in the Church of England the following year, he threw himself into the itinerant preaching that was to be his life's work. By all accounts he must have been a highly gifted orator – not only able to hold the attention of huge crowds, but also capable of swaying the most cultured and cynical of hearers. So great was his reputation that if an informed outsider had been asked, around the middle of the century, who was the founder of 'Methodism', the answer might well have been Whitefield, rather than Wesley. Whitefield's preaching led to the formation of a network of congregations under his general leadership, including two major chapels in London, in Moorfields and in Tottenham Court Road. The Moorfields chapel, like some of Whitefield's chapels in other parts of the country, was called a 'Tabernacle', and his congregations were often known by the collective title of the 'Tabernacle Connexion'. In some ways Whitefield's connexion mirrored that of Lady Huntingdon. But he spread himself too thinly (including making seven trips across the Atlantic to preach in America) to be able to weld his congregations into a cohesive organization.

The next conversion of a Holy Club member who was subsequently to establish a 'connexion' of his own was that of Benjamin Ingham in 1737. Ingham began preaching in Yorkshire in the late 1730s, and formed a small network of congregations and 'exhorters' – a group which he later sought to link with the Moravians. That decision helped ensure that his overall contribution to the Evangelical Revival was comparatively minor. Nevertheless, he remains noteworthy as another instance of a charismatic individual establishing his own denomination. Other such groups were to appear as the century went on.

Interestingly, the Wesleys' conversion experience in 1738 came after that of the two Holy Club colleagues just described. John's conversion did not lessen the concern for the pursuit of holiness that had been (and was to remain) a guiding principle of his religious life. Rather, it gave him a sense of being in personal receipt of God's favour. God welcomed the holiness attained by the believer, but his favour was not dependent upon it. It was Whitefield who first persuaded John to preach out of doors, and thus started him on the path that led to the emergence of Wesleyan Methodism. John does not seem to have had Whitefield's gifts as an orator, but he had far greater leadership and organizational skills – which is one reason why his version of Methodism emerged as such a dominant force.

The various evangelical groups that we have just described operated in parallel with the Church of England – not initially outside the Church, but nevertheless as distinct entities. As we shall see, the same was the case with Lady Huntingdon's Connexion. There were, however, individuals in the Church of England who embraced evangelical beliefs, but who saw no need to be part of any alternative organization themselves. They found no contradiction in being both Anglican and evangelical – indeed, they believed that when the Church was faithful to its own principles, it *was* evangelical. What they wanted, above all, was to convert the Church from within, and to restore it to what they saw as its true condition. In spreading their message, they might be careless about sticking within their own parish boundaries. And some evangelical clergy were prepared to assist the various external groups that we have been describing. (Lady Huntingdon's Connexion would not have got off the ground without the contribution made by such men.) But what is important to recognize is that the evangelical party in the Church of England was neither an offshoot nor a reflection of Wesley's Methodism or Whitefield's Methodism: it was an independent development, and a significant aspect of the Revival in its own right. But for this fact, it is unlikely that evangelicals would have become as distinct an entity within the Church of England as they had become by the start of the nineteenth century.

It was a similar situation within Dissent, where evangelical beliefs and practices also developed independently of the main Revival. An outstanding example of this was the Dissenter Philip Doddridge, teacher and hymn-writer, who as early as 1730 called on his fellow ministers to be 'evangelical and experimental' – by which he meant both to preach evangelical doctrines and to enable their converts to feel the impact of those doctrines in their hearts. Some Dissenters (like some Anglicans) were hostile to the Revival – either because they mistrusted the wilder implications of some evangelical teachings, or because they feared that evangelicals would steal their congregations (as they did). And some Dissenters resented the fact that revival was happening through a movement in which Anglicans had played a major part. But there were more friendly attitudes as well, and the relationship was two-way. The orthodoxy of the Revival was just what some Dissenting congregations were looking for, and so was its success in attracting congregations. So there were invitations to evangelical ministers to serve Dissenting chapels. At the same time, Dissenting ministers occasionally helped out evangelical groups, and some evangelical congregations ended up as fully-fledged Dissenters. This is what was to happen with a number of the congregations established by Lady Huntingdon's Connexion.

The result of all this interaction was that the Revival contributed significantly to the resurgence in Dissent that occurred during the eighteenth century.

We have so far described these different groups – evangelical Anglicans and evangelical Dissenters, as well as the various 'Methodist' groups that operated separately – as though they all shared a common theological position. To a large extent that is true: they would all have accepted the description of evangelical beliefs set out at the start of this chapter. But in one crucial respect Wesleyans differed from virtually all groups within the Revival, and it is worth noticing the broad outlines of the issue at this stage. It concerned free-will, and the extent to which individuals can contribute in any way to their own salvation. Most sections of the Revival held the theology generally termed 'Calvinist'. They were so convinced of God's absolute sovereignty, and so overwhelmed by his gracious kindness in granting them salvation, that they were not prepared to allow anything to diminish the wonder of what God had done. Since no-one could ever earn salvation, those who were saved must have been picked out by God in advance – predestined – to receive this special favour. For Wesley and those who thought like him (the term generally used to describe them was 'Arminian'), this made God into a capricious tyrant, selecting individuals for salvation or damnation on a whim. There must be some room for individuals to choose or reject salvation, said Arminians. No, said Calvinists, because that would make human choice superior to God's sovereign will. It would mean that salvation still had to be earned; it would cease to be a free gift, and the whole point of the gospel would be lost.

Each side was vulnerable to the other's attacks, since theological 'systems' of this sort can rarely be completely watertight. The Calvinists, in particular, were open to the charge that their doctrines encouraged moral laxity. If salvation did not depend on good behaviour (the argument ran), why bother to be good? Indeed, if you did try to be good, that might imply you thought you could earn salvation – so was it not better to sin, in order to emphasize how loving God was in still saving you? That line of reasoning is called antinomianism, meaning 'not subject to law'. Although few of the mainstream evangelicals accepted that this was the implication of their teaching, accusations of antinomianism were thrown around in the heat of controversy. And sometimes such beliefs were to be found on the fringes – even some of Lady Huntingdon's preachers, for example, found it a rather convenient doctrine to use with reluctant young women in their congregations!

John Wesley added a further dimension to this debate, with the doctrine known as Christian (or Sinless) Perfection. At the heart of his teaching, throughout his life, was the need for holiness. Even though believers were *saved* by faith, they had continually to battle against the remnants of sin within themselves. And Wesley believed that some Christians would achieve victory over those remnants of sin, even on this side of the grave.

These are all deep issues, and they have been around for most of Christian history. They were to surface dramatically during the eighteenth-century Revival, ranging the Wesleyans on one side and almost all the other groups – Anglican and Dissenting evangelicals, the Welsh Methodists, and connexions like Whitefield's and Lady Huntingdon's – on the other. They add one more ingredient to the rich medley that makes up the Evangelical Revival.

It is now time to consider how Lady Huntingdon fitted into this complex world, and the particular contribution she made to it.

3

Lady Huntingdon's Early Life
and Marriage

The future Countess of Huntingdon was born Selina Shirley on 24 August 1707. She was an aristocrat herself, being a daughter of the 2nd Earl Ferrers, who owned estates in Northamptonshire and Leicestershire. We do not know much about her early life, although its circumstances suggest that it may not have been particularly happy. The Ferrers were what would now be called a dysfunctional family, with rifts between various branches, and lawsuits that affected Selina and her sisters over a long period. Added to that, her parents were separated, and she was estranged from her mother for much of her life – an unhappy experience that was later to be repeated in respect of one of her own daughters.

Selina became Countess of Huntingdon in 1728, with her marriage to a near neighbour in Leicestershire, Theophilus Hastings, 9th Earl of Huntingdon, whose own country estate was Donnington Park near Ashby. The Huntingdon peerage was much older than the Ferrers's, and the family was richer, so the marriage must have appeared a good match. And it was a family where religion was taken seriously. This was especially the case with two of the Earl's sisters, Margaret and Frances, and with his half-sister Lady Betty Hastings, who had played an influential part in his early life. Lady Betty may not have agreed with all aspects of the Revival, but this did not prevent her from providing financial support for Whitefield and other early Methodists at Oxford. It seems quite likely that Lady Huntingdon's religious development – of which we have no definitive knowledge prior to her marriage – received an important stimulus from her new in-laws.

As well as being a good match in material terms, Selina's marriage to Lord Huntingdon seems to have been happy, indeed passionate. We know this (paradoxically) because the couple spent significant periods of time apart, and we can read some of the letters they sent to each other. Lady Huntingdon's absences were mainly due to her poor health, which was not helped by frequent pregnancies, and she made lengthy trips to Bath and other health resorts in pursuit of cures. Lord Huntingdon called her his 'Lady Leney' and his 'old goody'. She, in turn, wrote of longing to be back 'in the arms of my dear love', and once told him:

> I ever loved you to an excess of passion but since my absence from you I have felt greater pains than I ever thought that [separation was] capable of giving, and I hope in God I shall return to my dearest of lives by the first week in April.

Lady Huntingdon to Lord Huntingdon, 19 February 1731/2. HMC, iii, 10.

The marriage lasted only 18 years, ending with the Earl's sudden death in 1746. It was said that to the end of Lady Huntingdon's long life – she survived him by some 45 years – she still wept at the mention of his name. She was equally devoted to her children – her 'little Jewels' as she called them – but here too there was to be sadness. Of her four sons and three daughters, only her daughter Elizabeth outlived her. And it was from Elizabeth that she became estranged: mother and daughter apparently did not meet at all in the last decades of Lady Huntingdon's life. Part of the problem may have been Elizabeth's refusal to adopt her mother's religious principles, and this was also a factor behind the coolness that developed between Lady Huntingdon and the only other one of her children to live a significant adult life. This was her eldest son

Francis, who succeeded his father as 10th Earl of Huntingdon, but died in 1789. In Francis's case, she had not helped her cause by placing his further education under the guidance of the cultivated but worldly Lord Chesterfield. She could hardly have been unaware that Chesterfield was about the last person to turn to, if one wanted a young man to turn out a pious evangelical. It almost seems she took less care over Francis's religious development than she did about his assuming his proper place in English society. If so, she paid the price. In Lady Huntingdon's later years, congregations and individual ministers quite often called her their 'Mother in Israel'; she may well have reflected on the irony of this, set against her loss, by death or estrangement, of those whose real mother she was.

Apart from being a devoted wife and mother, what sort of woman was the young Countess in the early years of her marriage? The answer is that she was something of a mixture. She was certainly not a pious fugitive from fashionable society. She and her husband lived the life and the lifestyle expected of their rank in society, and this could include spending lavishly on clothes – on one occasion, Lady Huntingdon ordered over 20 yards 'of the most exceeding beautiful Silk of many colours' to be bought for her in Paris. She also took a close interest in their different homes. As well as their country estate in Leicestershire, the Huntingdons leased various houses in and around London: for a time they had a house in Savile Row – later replaced by the lease of 11 Downing Street – and an out-of-town retreat at Enfield Chase. In 1745 they added a house in Chelsea. In her attitude to her houses, we can see the same authoritarianism and concern for practical details that were later to mark the running of her Connexion. While the Enfield house was being adapted, she wrote to her husband:

> I came here and hurried the workmen to such a degree that I believe they wish my absence almost as much as I do myself.

Were my life with me I should think it the most delightful place under heaven.

Lady Huntingdon to Lord Huntingdon, 6 September 1734. HMC, iii, 19.

Money, it seems, was an important preoccupation. The Huntingdons were outraged, for example, when they discovered that they had not benefited as they had hoped from the death of Lady Betty Hastings in 1739. It also appears, from her correspondence with friends, that Lady Huntingdon took a close interest in society gossip, and that she played an active part in the season when she was at Bath. And loyal wife though she was, she was evidently so high-spirited on one occasion that a friend warned her not to 'coquette' with a particular noble lord, because the friend wanted him for herself.

Another aspect of Lady Huntingdon's interest in the outside world concerned the political sphere. In 1738 she gave a dramatic demonstration of the strength of her interest. In that year she was one of a group of peeresses who mounted an all-day siege on the gallery of the House of Lords, in an attempt to gain access to a particular debate. In the end, they tricked the House authorities into thinking they had given up and left: when the gallery doors were unlocked, the women stormed in and got their seats.

Sometimes Lady Huntingdon was the one who was in London, while her husband was elsewhere. When this happened, she kept him informed of developments and showed her relish for political gossip:

... public affairs are in the utmost confusion. There will be above twenty [government] changes ... The *great man* will speak to nobody. Lord Ches[terfield] goes to Ireland by choice, to be out of the way of Pel[ha]m's scraps and to be sure of a good place. [The] Duke of Bedford is to be at the head of the Admiralty. Lord C[artere]t went to see Lord Orford after he had been to see Lord Harrington and told the former that he had been to worship the rising sun and he was now come to see the setting sun.

Lady Huntingdon to Lord Huntingdon, 8 December 1744. HMC, iii, 48.

Lord Huntingdon did not play an active part in the House of Lords, but he and his wife do seem to have had long-standing Jacobite sympathies. Whether they should be counted as active *supporters* of Bonnie Prince Charlie is more difficult to say. They certainly included some staunch Jacobites within their circle, and they followed closely the events of the 1745 uprising – including the subsequent trial in the House of Lords of the Jacobite nobles who had taken part. Lord Huntingdon had a difficult job convincing his peers that his absence from the trial was for genuine reasons of ill health. This in itself suggests that some people doubted his loyalty, and there are signs that Lady Huntingdon was also regarded as suspect in some quarters. She sent her husband an account of the trial, and showed her sympathy for those condemned to death:

There seems to be no hopes for any escaping of the three lords. The King thinks he has fully answered Lord Cromartie's plea by having promised to take care of his family . . .

. . . Lord Balmerino's behaviour is so much approved of by all; most of all opinions wish for him most as so brave and so honest a man . . .

. . . The uncommon greatness of Dawson's and Flether's reasons for not applying . . . for their lives, I think, ought to be remembered. Had they been obliged (they both declared) to the E[lector] of H[anover] for their lives, the obligation must have been so great as for ever to have prevented their defending a cause they believed just, and therefore did not desire life upon those conditions.

Lady Huntingdon to Lord Huntingdon, August 1746. HMC, iii, 61.

Lady Huntingdon was later to have links with the 'opposition' to George II's government that formed around the Prince of Wales. But on the intriguing question of whether she was actively disloyal during the 'Forty-five', the evidence is no more than circumstantial.

The picture that emerges of Lady Huntingdon during these years is of a pretty normal, if high-spirited and hot-tempered, young noblewoman. But a more serious side was apparent, even before her conversion. Despite her active participation in society, there were definite limits to her interest and tolerance: she was, for example, shocked by instances of sexual impropriety, and in 1732 she described the grand ball in Bath as 'to my way of thinking . . . very stupid'. There is also evidence of active philanthropy, including support for a school at Melbourne in Derbyshire, for Coram's Foundling Hospital, and for the SPCK. From time to time she made significant purchases of Bibles, Prayer Books and other items, so that it seems likely she was helping religious activities of some sort.

So we have a passionate individual, but one with a serious and religious side to her character. These two aspects of her personality made a powerful mix when she went through her conversion experience in 1739.

4

Conversion

⟡

We do not in fact know a great deal about the events surrounding Lady Huntingdon's conversion. Unlike John Wesley, she left no account either of the preceding circumstances, or of how her religious outlook changed afterwards. Was it, for example, a full-blown evangelical conversion like Wesley's, giving her a personal sense of forgiveness and acceptance by God? Or was it, at this stage, simply a resolution to make religion a more central part of her life? What we do know, however, is that her sister-in-law Margaret Hastings had already passed through a conversion experience of some kind, through the influence of Benjamin Ingham. Margaret spoke freely of the happiness this had brought her, and this may well have had an impact on Lady Huntingdon. We know also that the key date for her was June/ July 1739, when she was recovering from a period of illness, and was pregnant with her last child.

The person to whom Lady Huntingdon turned initially for spiritual advice was the Revd Thomas Barnard, who was Master of the Leeds Grammar School and a confidant of Lady Betty Hastings. This is fortunate from our point of view, since his surviving letters to Lady Huntingdon provide a few clues as to her spiritual state. She had told him, for example, that she had 'taken herself to the life of religion', a decision that came as no surprise to Barnard, since he had previously thought her 'close to the Kingdom of Heaven'. This is a pretty clear sign that her conversion came as the climax of a period of reflection and preparation, rather than out of the blue.

Barnard quickly disappears from our story (possibly because the Huntingdons suspected him of influencing Lady Betty's decision not to leave her estate to them), but for a brief spell he acted as a wise counsellor to Lady Huntingdon. He clearly recognized the impulsiveness and introspection that were to remain key features of her volatile personality. His prescription was:

- That your Ladyship would observe moderation in all things; nor be hurried on with too much eagerness in the spiritual combat; . . . nor fall into discouragement and despondency for any slips . . . you may make.
- That your Ladyship would admit but very few to any knowledge . . . of the business you have in hand, nor make any discovery of it by any violent changes in outward appearances . . .
- That you would hold all your passions, as joy, grief, desire, fear etc out of extremes . . .
- That your exercises of prayer & meditation be not too laborious, nor bear too hard upon your strength.

Thomas Barnard to Lady Huntingdon, 28 July 1739. DE23/1/1428, LRO.

Lord Huntingdon appears to have been indulgent of his wife's new religious zeal. He may even have shared in it to some degree, as his sisters clearly believed, although the evidence on this is not conclusive. Others of Lady Huntingdon's family were not so tolerant. Her younger sister Mary, with whom she now differed as part of the long-running dispute over their father's estate, was scathing about the clouded judgement that Selina's faith had brought her – not to mention the 'Canting set of people' with whom she was now associated. Whether conversion had a beneficial effect on her character is hard to say. One visitor in late 1740 was told by her maid (and who should know better?) that she 'has not been a passion for more than twelve months' – yet the visitor himself still thought that Lady Huntingdon displayed a 'choleric and violent temper'.

The visitor in question was James Hutton, a London book-seller and a leading figure among the Moravians in England. The fact that Lady Huntingdon had such Moravian contacts is interesting, because there was a distinct Moravian element in the early days of her new faith. This resulted initially from Margaret Hastings's decision to send Ingham down to see her at Donnington – and the fact that Ingham was by now closely asso-ciated with the Moravians. Lady Huntingdon's support was soon sought, and secured, for Moravian missionary projects, includ-ing their orphanage at Herrenhaag near Frankfurt. In the spring of 1740 she had the idea of looking for a doctor with Moravian beliefs to live in her household and minister to the poor of the area. Not too much should be read into these early links with the Moravians, however. The Revival was still very fluid at this stage, with the various 'parties' we examined in chapter 2 only very loosely distinguished – sometimes, indeed, with no sharp distinction in people's minds between evangelical beliefs and other 'serious' expressions of Christian faith. (An example of this was Margaret Hastings, who recommended that her brother read the interesting combination of Whitefield's sermons and Jeremy Taylor's *Holy Living*, and told her sister-in-law she expected her to benefit from an anticipated visit from William Law.)

Lady Huntingdon was, in any case, soon to be estranged from the Moravians. The original grounds for this were not theologi-cal, but the fact that in 1740 Margaret's relations with Ingham had taken a romantic turn. The Huntingdons' hostility to the pro-posed marriage was largely based on the couple's different social status: the fact, in the words of one aristocratic commentator, that Margaret had 'disposed of herself to a poor wandering methodist'. It did not help, either, that Margaret's marriage would mean that she benefited by an extra £3,000 from a provision of Lady Betty's will. But marry they eventually did, in November 1741.

It is striking that alienation from the Moravians, her early source of spiritual support, did not lead Lady Huntingdon to abandon her new faith. Clearly its roots went deep. And by 1741, if not earlier, she had established a new link with the Revival, in the form of friendship with the Wesleys. Given the stormy nature of Lady Huntingdon's later relationship with John Wesley, it is interesting that their initial contacts seem to have been so warm. The frequency of the visits that John made to her at Enfield Chase in 1741, and the hours they spent in discussion, suggest that these were not mere counselling sessions, but more of an exchange between equals about the faith and how it should be spread.

By this stage, moreover, divisions had begun to appear within the new movement. The first of these affected John Wesley's relations with the Moravians. Moravians had played an important part in Wesley's religious development, and his first Methodist Society – at Fetter Lane in London – had been something of a joint venture with them. Strains between Wesley and the more extreme Moravian elements at Fetter Lane, however, had led in 1740 to the Wesleyan group decamping to new premises at the Foundry in Moorfields. The principal cause of the dispute was the belief, held by some Moravians, that was known as 'stillness'. The idea was that only perfect faith counted as faith at all, and that until one achieved such faith, one should remain 'still' – that is, take no part in worship or the sacraments. Wesley reacted strongly against this idea. Lady Huntingdon likewise remained firm in the face of attempts by certain Moravians to argue her into the stillness camp, and during 1741 she was active in persuading Charles Wesley not to join them either. This is an instructive sign of how quickly she assumed an authority role within the Revival. Later in the decade, when she was recently widowed, she was attracted for a while by beliefs not dissimilar from Moravian 'stillness'. But there appear to have been no further formal contacts with the Moravians, apart from a short-lived attempt at reconciliation in the early 1760s.

The period immediately following Lady Huntingdon's conversion also saw the first dispute within the Revival over belief in predestination. As we saw in chapter 2, these are profound and difficult questions, and ones that arise almost inevitably when evangelicals start to talk about grace and salvation. The issue came into the open in 1740, when a pamphlet war broke out between Whitefield and Wesley. It was not until late 1742 that a measure of peace was restored between them. The interesting thing is that at this stage Lady Huntingdon was firmly in the Wesley camp, including being fully convinced about Christian Perfection. When she met Whitefield by chance in 1742, she rejected his arguments for predestination, and told him of the hope that Perfection gave her:

> ... he held forth above two hours upon the doctrine of election and reprobation ... telling withal (or giving me to understand) I was an elect. I told him ... I should be such a loser by his way [of] thinking [&] that no consideration that I was yet able to see from anything he had said could have any weight ... I told him I was so much happier than he was & that not from anything in myself but on my constant dependence upon Christ, & [trusted him for] an absolute deliverance from [?sin]. He then said 'pray does your Ladyship live without sin?' I told him no, but that there was such a state ... & that before we died it was absolutely necessary we should be in it.

> Lady Huntingdon to John or Charles Wesley, 19 February 1742. Meth. Arch. CHV 3.

Lady Huntingdon continued for some time to regard John Wesley warmly. In April 1742, she told him:

> Nothing less I look for from you than making our apostate Church the footstool of Christ. For this end was you born & for this end came you & your brother into this world. Attempt nothing less than all mankind ... all will fall before you, I know it. I am sure of it. You are the only one, with your brother, that has ever showed the riches of the Gospel & God will open more & more to you.

> Lady Huntingdon to John Wesley, 29 April 1742. Meth. Arch. CHV 107.

In the course of that year, however, she was to shift her principal allegiance from John to Charles – a friendship that survived many (though not all) of the strains of her later relationship with John. Perhaps she recognized, even then, that John saw her as a challenge to his authority. For the moment, however, Lady Huntingdon was still firmly on the Arminian side of the Revival. In 1743 she had a seat permanently reserved for her at Wesley's West Street chapel in London – an arrangement proposed by Charles, though one that John thought showed her too much respect! But by the following year she was tiring of the idea of Perfection, and moving towards predestination. She had begun friendly contacts with George Whitefield, and started attending his London Tabernacle. She also forged links with the (Calvinist) Welsh lay preacher Howell Harris. The religious alignments were taking shape that would govern the rest of her life.

These theological issues apart, what role did Lady Huntingdon play in the Revival in the years following her conversion? We have noted in passing that she began to use her influence and authority from early on, and there were continuing instances of this. She made known to the Wesleys her views for and against various publishing initiatives; she had some influence over John Wesley's choice of preaching areas, including, most notably, his mission to the Newcastle miners in 1743; and in the following year she played host at her London house to those attending the first Methodist conference. She could be a source of spiritual advice, as well as a recipient. She encouraged the young preacher Thomas Maxfield to exercise his ministerial gifts, for example, and Harris acknowledged the spiritual benefits he had obtained from discussions with her. She learned quickly, as well, that her social position could be used to assist or defend the new movement. So she supported attempts to secure ordination for a man lacking in formal qualifications, and she was consulted by a congregation having difficulty with their local magistrate. In 1745, against the backdrop of the Jacobite rising, she aided efforts to convince the regime that the new movement was not disloyal to the House of Hanover.

Lady Huntingdon was also involved, in the years immediately following her conversion, in more direct and practical forms of Christian service. She had various plans for schools, including one which the master would combine with selling Wesley's publications. The distribution of religious literature was in fact an important part of her ministry. In 1746 she arranged for some of William Law's works to be printed – probably for free distribution, like the Wesley works that she appears previously to have had reprinted. She took an interest in how the Revival was spreading across the country: when Charles Wesley was in Cornwall in 1743, for example, she sent him a gift for the Methodists in St Ives. She prayed and read with her own servants (not necessarily with their agreement!) and she asked John Wesley if it would be in order for her to expound the Scriptures to them. She used her family chaplain to run 'a little meeting' in her house, and there were schemes to address the physical and spiritual needs of the poor of the neighbourhood. Her ministry was direct and personal:

> God shows forth his love & power every moment among us & we find many added to the believers. My poor old woman is quite recovered ... [and] very faithful to that which is committed to her ... I have laboured much among the unawakened. I let none pass by of any rank ... God blesses my labours for their bodily health so much that they come many miles to me on that account & many God sends home a seeking him ... I am brought by reading, singing & talking to them almost past opening my mouth.
>
> Lady Huntingdon to Charles Wesley, n.d. (stamped 16 August). Meth. Arch. CHV 84.

Sometimes she urged her message with such force that, as she herself recognized, many were frightened off.

The Huntingdons were still playing their part in the secular world, and Lady Huntingdon regarded this as an opportunity for evangelism. Thus she rejoiced at the chance to work 'amongst the fine Ladys at Bath' – but on another occasion lamented that she had not found the right words to witness to the company who were with them. Once Howell Harris was in her orbit, she got him to preach to friends gathered at her house. Some of the Huntingdons' circle were resistant, however, to her enthusiastic promotion of her new faith. One of the women who joined a small group that Lady Huntingdon gathered in London was forbidden by her husband to see the Countess any more. On another occasion, a dinner guest declined fish with the comment that he would have made a bad Romanist, since he could neither eat fish nor pray ten times a day – a comment that Lady Huntingdon and the other guests interpreted as directed at her. (For Lady Huntingdon the incident had a highly satisfactory outcome, since at that very moment the man's servant appeared to fall dead on the floor. The man recovered after an hour, so Lady Huntingdon was convinced this was a sign from God to his sceptical master.)

Despite all this activity, there was a darker side to Lady Huntingdon's life, during these final years while Lord Huntingdon was alive. She dreaded outliving her husband, and his declining health in the final months of his life – possibly linked with some form of depressive illness – must have caused her much grief. The Huntingdons had already had to bear the deaths from smallpox of two of their sons, as well as the death in infancy of a daughter. Added to this, there were continuing disputes over wills on both sides of the family. Sadly it does not seem that Lady Huntingdon's new faith brought her consistent peace of mind, and there is a good deal of soul-searching and self-loathing in her letters during this period:

> You visited me in the time of my distress, but you nor no soul can conceive the darkness, perplexity, misery I have [which]

constantly surrounds me. It is what I have never felt since I was known of God . . .

. . . If you have one grain of charity for me, it must be because . . . you will not let [her] know how worthless a worm she is who knows herself more obliged to you than to any creature living. I would pray for you if I could, but I cannot for anything but that God would have mercy upon the chief of sinners.

Lady Huntingdon to (?) Charles Wesley, 1743. Meth. Arch. CHV 13.

There is even a story that her religious distress became so great, at one stage after her conversion, that some of the Earl's friends advised that he should have her committed to an asylum – but he had too much affection for her to do so.

Lady Huntingdon herself occasionally thought of some form of escape from the world. She once described to Charles Wesley her vision of founding a utopian community, a town against which the gates of hell could not prevail, and in which God's people could live safely and faithfully together. This idea was not entirely original. It may have owed something to the community that formed at Little Gidding in the previous century, or to the 'settlements' which the Moravians had established in various parts of Britain – and which also inspired the 'Family' which Howell Harris founded at Trevecka in 1752. (Harris saw his community as a refuge from the world, and compared it to the inn in the parable of the Good Samaritan.) Had Lady Huntingdon given way to her daydreams, she might not have initiated the work for which she is now remembered. But that work still lay a good way in the future, during the long years of her widowhood.

5

Widowhood and Its Aftermath

❧

Lord Huntingdon died on 13 October 1746, aged 49. He was buried in the parish church at Ashby-de-la-Zouch. Strikingly, it was Lord Bolingbroke – a staunch opponent of the government, but also a sceptic in regard to revealed religion – who was asked to compose the lengthy inscription that appears on his tomb. Francis, the Huntingdons' eldest child, was still four years away from coming of age when his father died. This meant that the whole responsibility for the children (two of whom, Selina and Henry, were still under ten), as well as management of the family's complex financial affairs, devolved entirely onto Lady Huntingdon. It was not until after the tragically early deaths of Henry and Selina, in 1758 and 1763 respectively, that she was finally free of domestic constraints.

An early issue for Lady Huntingdon was how far she should continue and develop her religious role. Her views fluctuated a great deal. Four months after her husband's death, she expressed her fear of losing the momentum she had previously built up. She dreaded, she said, 'slack hands in the vineyard; we must all be up and doing'. A few weeks later, however, she was less sure. After Howell Harris had preached to an aristocratic gathering in her house, she

consulted me about which was best, to live retired and give up all, or fill her place, and I said the latter I thought was right whilst she felt she was enabled to be faithful and felt the Lord was with her.

Howell Harris's Diary for 9 April 1747. *Howell Harris's Visits to London*, p. 137.

We are reminded of how Lady Huntingdon had previously dreamed of a retreat from the world. That sentiment did not go away, and the following year she contemplated retiring to the family's house in Ashby, in order to be near her husband's grave. Such feelings did not mean she was giving up on her faith. More likely they came at times when she was particularly drawn to the more mystical aspects of religion – that is, the desire for a direct sense of God, attained through personal experience. This fitted with the Quakers' belief in receiving inner illumination from God, and with the Moravian idea (which Lady Huntingdon had previously rejected) of waiting quietly for the Spirit to act. It was also the direction that William Law's thinking had taken. We have already noticed Lady Huntingdon's contacts with Law at the time of her conversion, and she continued to admire him. In 1749 Law published the first part of *The Spirit of Prayer*, a book influenced by long study of the seventeenth-century German mystic Jacob Boehme, who believed in direct divine illumination. Lady Huntingdon bought Law's book in bulk to give away to friends, and she was still using it as a tract in the mid 1750s.

Interest in mysticism was not good news, however, so far as more orthodox evangelicals were concerned. Wesley said of Law's book that it was 'lively and entertaining; but it is another gospel'. (Wesley objected to Law's saying that God was never angry. In that case, Wesley asked, why do we need Christ's sacrifice to reconcile us to God?) Moreover, placing too much reliance on the testimony of the Spirit – something that is notoriously difficult to interpret objectively – can undermine the authority of Scripture. This was what worried Harris about Lady Huntingdon's mystical interests, even though belief in direct divine inspiration was something to which evangelicals themselves were susceptible. In 1747 Harris thought that she was 'warping towards Quakerism and Mr Law', and he feared she was at risk of spiritual pride. That anxiety was not helped when he heard her

> speak of her entire deadness to her own will, and of the revelations she has from God. She mentioned how she is with and near the Lord continually without interruption.
>
> Howell Harris's Diary for 5 January 1748. *Howell Harris's Visits to London*, p. 171.

Despite this interest in mysticism, there seems never to have been any real threat that Lady Huntingdon would give up her evangelical faith. What those interests do suggest, however, is that she still found it difficult to steer between the various religious influences to which she was subjected. Maybe that inner confusion never really left her, even when she appeared totally convinced of the rightness of whatever course she was currently pursuing. Maybe it forced her to appear more certain than she really was. This, together with her naturally fiery temper, may explain the authoritarian streak that often made her a difficult and unpredictable person with whom to deal.

Whatever Lady Huntingdon's inner turmoil, the practice of her faith was already sufficiently well known to expose her to public hostility:

> Our affronts and persecutions here, for the word's sake, are hardly to be described ... They called out in the open streets for me, saying, if they had me they would tear me to pieces.
>
> Lady Huntingdon to Philip Doddridge, 21 May 1747. Nuttall, *Doddridge Calendar*, Letter 1241.

Dr Doddridge, the recipient of that letter, was one of the few prominent Dissenting ministers to be associated with the Revival at this early stage. His premature death, in 1751, deprived Lady Huntingdon of a wise friend, who might have provided her with steadying advice during some of the stormier years of her future ministry.

An important event took place in 1748, which was to bring that ministry a stage closer. This was the return to England of George Whitefield, who had been preaching in America since 1744. For a brief period he resumed the leadership of the English Calvinistic Methodists, but he had come back knowing that Lady Huntingdon was keen to work with him – and by implication he accepted the changes which this implied for his future ministry. She may even have been the reason for his return, in which case it shows what a considerable influence she was thought capable of wielding. She appointed him one of her official chaplains, having already begun to involve him in her work among the upper classes. Whitefield was probably the finest orator produced by the Revival, and the best known, so having him to speak in her house was a considerable draw. After the first occasion, she wrote excitedly to Doddridge:

> I must just tell you that I have had two large assemblies at my house of the mighty, the noble, the wise & the rich to hear the Gospel by Mr Whitefield & I have great pleasure in telling you they all expressed a great deal in hearing of him. Sometimes I do hope for Lord Chesterfield.
>
> Lady Huntingdon to Doddridge, 30 August 1748. Nuttall, *Doddridge Calendar*, Letter 1392.

Over time, an impressive cross-section of fashionable eighteenth-century society assembled in Lady Huntingdon's drawing rooms. No-one seems to have thought it at all surprising that such prominent sceptics about religion as Lords Chesterfield and Bolingbroke should have remained regular guests of Lady Huntingdon. The fact that old friends continued within her circle is testimony to the regard in which she was still held – as well, no doubt, to the skills of those she invited to preach.

It has to be said, however, that the results of Lady Huntingdon's upper-class ministry fell short of expectations. The hoped-for spate of conversions did not materialize, nor did the more strategic objective voiced by some in Lady Huntingdon's circle. This was the possibility that they might capitalize upon their links with the Prince of Wales to secure Whitefield's consecration as a bishop. This (probably faint) hope was dashed by the Prince's death in 1751, before he had acceded to the throne. It is interesting to speculate, however, how different the Evangelical Revival might have been if someone like Whitefield *had* become a bishop at this stage. It would probably have led, for example, to a lot more evangelical clergy being ordained. That, in turn, might have meant a much stronger evangelical party within the Church of England, relative to evangelicals outside. So far as Lady Huntingdon was concerned, it might have removed the need to start her training college. And without her college, she would not have had available the student manpower needed to develop her Connexion . . .

Whitefield flattered Lady Huntingdon, and from time to time he even hinted that she might assume a leadership role within the Revival:

> I rejoice in the prospect of seeing your Ladyship happy amidst a crowd of your spiritual children, who will come to you . . . to be built up in their most holy faith.

> Perhaps our Lord is fitting your Ladyship for some new work.

> A leader is wanting. This honour hath been put upon your Ladyship by the great head of the church. An honour conferred on few, but an earnest of a distinguished honour to be put upon your Ladyship before men and angels, when time shall be no more.

Whitefield to Lady Huntingdon, 28 January, 13 May and 30 November 1749. *Select Letters* (1772), ii, 225, 256, 294.

Those last words imply headship of a united movement. But neither Lady Huntingdon, nor anyone else, was to play such a role. It is difficult, indeed, to imagine that there could ever have been a single leader of the different strands of Methodism, even though the movement was barely a dozen years old. The theological divisions ran too deep: 'we are on two different plans', as Whitefield told Wesley in 1748. Among the individual leaders, however, there was a feeling that the Revival should at least appear more unified. Although Lady Huntingdon took no direct part in the negotiations that ensued between Whitefield, Harris and the Wesleys in 1749, she was closely involved in the preparatory discussions with Whitefield and Harris. That was a sign of the central place she now held in the movement, and also of the fact that she was now firmly identified with the Calvinists. The initiative led to an agreement on ways of preventing friction between the various wings of the Revival, including avoiding controversial subjects, and attempting to use each other's theological language as much as possible.

Interestingly, one of the issues that had been raised was Whitefield's objection to Wesley 'monopolising the name of Methodist to himself only'. It seems from this, and from the other reports of the discussions, that the focus had been on secondary issues, rather than on questions of deep theology. If so, that was a wise recognition that some areas of theology were incapable of being resolved by debate, however profound or prolonged – and that what mattered was living peacefully alongside one another. Unfortunately, the leaders of the Revival did not always remember this salutary lesson.

The rapprochement was symbolized by Wesley taking services with Whitefield and with Harris in January 1750. In the background to these attempts at reconciliation, however, there were personal animosities at work – animosities to which, paradoxically, rivalry for Lady Huntingdon's favour contributed. Although Harris had played a key role in bringing Whitefield and Lady

Huntingdon together in 1748, he was deeply hurt by the close bond that subsequently developed between them. He objected to Whitefield's assumed superiority, and thought (probably correctly) that he detected pride and self-interest in Whitefield's behaviour. Though alert to the failings of others, however, Harris was curiously blind to such traits in himself. The relevant passages from Harris's diary make an interesting contrast, as well as providing an insight into the hothouse atmosphere that had developed at the centre of the Revival:

> This morning I saw what I never did before, that I was head in this Reformation, viz. that no one is to control me to send me here or there ... but the Lord Himself.

Diary for 28 November 1749.

> [Whitefield] did not seem to me to honour me and the brethren as ministers, but rather to use us as gents do stewards.

Diary for 4 January 1750.

> The Lord ... showed ... my place to oversee Mr Whitefield and Wesley, to see that no self comes in.

Diary for 9 January 1750.

> When we came to the Countess, I saw [Whitefield's] spirit jumping over me, despised me and got beyond me in her heart ...

Diary for 5 September 1751 (reviewing the events of 1749 and 1750).

Howell Harris's Visits to London, pp. 247, 256, 259, 15.

It did not help matters when Whitefield joined in the general criticism of Harris's association (possibly innocent, possibly not) with a married woman. Harris was banned from preaching at Whitefield's London Tabernacle, and he withdrew to Wales to concentrate on his work there. He reappears later in the story of Lady Huntingdon, but he remained permanently estranged from Whitefield.

Strikingly, Harris had warmed towards Wesley, as he cooled to Whitefield – another reminder that theology sometimes mattered less than more basic emotions. Harris respected the fact that Wesley (unlike Whitefield) continued to preach at 'little places', and not just to the elite. Wesley himself was complimentary about Harris's preaching. Did Wesley, like Harris, resent Whitefield's appointment as Lady Huntingdon's chaplain? Certainly neither of the Wesleys had ever been offered that honour. But nor, prior to this, had anyone else of comparable standing within the Revival. Being chaplain to a peeress was relatively unimportant in itself. It only mattered because of what Whitefield made of it, and for what it signified about the future direction of his (and her) work. Within a few months – and possibly under her influence – he had again given up leadership of the Calvinistic Methodists, preferring to focus upon broad goals, like the conversion of the nation and of the national church, rather than simply to nurture a sect.

It is hard to imagine that John Wesley would ever have considered relinquishing control of his societies like this. Still less would he have felt at home being even nominally subservient to Lady Huntingdon, in the way that service as her chaplain implied. There was no open breach between them, though there are already hints of the friction that characterized their relationship to the end of their long lives. She often seemed suspicious of him, while he found her both erratic and dictatorial. Early in 1748, for example, she made the strange (and unexplained) remark that she 'feared him of all men in the world'. Observers believed that her growing regard for Whitefield was prejudicing her against Wesley. That, however, did not prevent her, later in the year, from badgering Wesley to visit her – not once, but three times in the space of less than a week. In his private Diary (though not his *Journal*) Wesley was candid about his reluctance:

Being not able with tolerable decency to excuse myself any longer, I went to Chelsea and spent two or three hours as in the times that are past. I hoped one journey would serve. But I was too hasty in reckoning. LH pressed me to come again on Friday, so that I could not handsomely decline it.

I took up my cross once more, and came to Chelsea . . . There was a consequence I was not aware of. She begged [me] to come once more.

About eight I reached Chelsea . . .

Wesley's Diary for 7, 9 and 11 September 1748, *Journal*, viii, 157 & 158.

Much of Wesley's visits to Chelsea consisted of preaching to titled guests, but there was also an opportunity for private conversation with Lady Huntingdon. During the latter, Wesley – in a chilling but characteristic expression – 'delivered my own soul'. That is a phrase, like 'speaking the truth in love', which can sometimes be used to justify hurtful criticism. On this occasion, however, Lady Huntingdon 'received it well, the tears standing in her eyes'.

Behind such contacts, the incipient tensions between John Wesley and Lady Huntingdon can already be discerned. But at this stage in their lives, those tensions were not so rigid as to prevent any contact or collaboration between them.

Much had happened to Lady Huntingdon in the decade since her conversion. She had moved from the role of new convert, seeking to understand the implications of the faith she had embraced, to that of an uninhibited defender of that faith at the highest levels of society. She had lost the husband who had been the principal object of her sometimes fiery emotions – and had now found a substitute emotional life in the drama of evangelical religion, with its language of light and darkness, salvation or perdition. She had established contacts with a band of religious leaders whose extrovert personalities matched the starkness of the gospel they taught. At the same time, the theological shifts through which she had passed during the 1740s suggest (even if they do not prove) an uncertain and insecure personality. Those were the same traits that were to inhibit planning, and blight friendships, during the decades that followed.

In Lady Huntingdon's activities during the late 1740s and early 1750s, we can see some of the main themes that were to mark her life in the years ahead. Four in particular stand out. One was her direct involvement in ministry, whether in the drawing room among her peers, or in the form of charity and mission to the poor. Another was public defence of Methodism and its adherents, both leaders and local congregations. (In 1750 she secured a notable victory over the then Bishop of Exeter, when she extracted an apology from him for false accusations he had made against Wesley and Whitefield.) A third theme was help and support for those seeking ordination – which is notable when one considers the active interest she was later to take in ministerial formation and education.

Fourth, and perhaps of greatest potential significance, was the visible role she had assumed within the movement. She was still far from having established anything that could be called a connexion of her own. But that, in itself, should have been a strength. Without personal interests to defend, she was well placed to be protector and counsellor to all sections of the Revival. In a movement where personal egos played so significant a part, she could, with the right inclination and self-discipline, have been a force for moderation and mutual tolerance. It is interesting to speculate on the longer-term influence she might have exercised, had she not become identified with (and encumbered by) a sect of her own.

6

The 1750s: Lady Huntingdon's Circle Expands

༺༄༂༅༆༺

One might have supposed that by the start of the 1750s Lady Huntingdon would have formed a reasonable idea of the contribution she could make to the Revival. We have seen the different ways in which she was already involved, so the next stage should have been to draw these strands together into a coherent strategy.

The evidence, however, is that she was still in a fair state of perplexity. One sign of this was her rooted conviction, early in 1751, that she had breast cancer – a fixation that the reassurance of her medical advisers was unable to dispel. Once again Lady Huntingdon was nagged by uncertainty as to whether she should retreat from the world, or continue an active role within the church. This time the 'darkness' lasted some two years from 1750, and could have been one of the reasons why she apparently gave up her meetings of nobility at her Chelsea home from that year. There were also external factors to distress her. The year 1751 saw the death of her sister-in-law Frances Hastings, and also the deteriorating health of her wise friend Philip Doddridge. Doddridge was gravely ill with consumption by the summer of 1751. Lady Huntingdon took a close interest in his care, and was instrumental in raising several hundred pounds to send him to Lisbon in September, in an attempt to improve his condition. She even thought of going with him. Her efforts proved in vain, however, and Doddridge died within a short time of his arrival in Portugal.

Lady Huntingdon had further changes to contend with, so far as her ministerial friends were concerned. We have seen already how Whitefield had effectively displaced Harris in her special favour, provoking the latter to withdraw to Wales. Lady Huntingdon could not realistically have imagined that Whitefield would remain permanently at her beck and call in London, even though she was providing him with substantial sums of money. Whatever her actual expectations, he was soon back on the road as an itinerant preacher, visiting all corners of the British Isles during the course of 1750, and making a short return to America in 1751–52. We do not know how Lady Huntingdon felt about sharing Whitefield with the world in this way, though there is evidence later on that she resented it when he developed links with other aristocratic women.

Lady Huntingdon was developing a new clerical contact, however, in the person of Charles Wesley. Lady Huntingdon had earlier played an important part in Charles's life by effectively underwriting the financial arrangements agreed with Charles's future father-in-law, as a condition for permitting his daughter Sally's marriage to Charles in 1749. Thereafter there was a rift of some kind between Lady Huntingdon and Charles, followed by a reconciliation in 1751. That rapprochement was so warm that Charles soon felt able to write frankly to her about his resentment at his brother's domination over him – a letter which somehow found itself into John's hands, and led to a caustic response. It cannot have helped John's longer-term attitude towards Lady Huntingdon to see his brother using her as his confidante in this way. The tension between the brothers continued, with John resentful that Charles took more notice of Lady Huntingdon than of him, in deciding where he should preach. In 1753 there was a further example of the closeness between Charles and Lady Huntingdon, when she nursed Sally through smallpox. Charles was away during this crisis, and in her letters to him she comes over as a wise and compassionate friend – as she did, soon after, when the couple lost a child to the same disease. One biographer of Lady Huntingdon has commented on her propensity to 'adopt' clerical couples, and she was certainly very close to Charles and Sally Wesley at this stage, exchanging letters, gifts and visits with them. The warmth of their relationship contrasts markedly with the reserve that can be detected in her attitude to John.

There were other changes in her life in the early 1750s. Her eldest son came of age in March 1750, though this did not mean much relief from family business, since Francis had by then departed on an extended Grand Tour that kept him abroad until 1756. We do not know how early in Francis's adolescence he began to diverge from his mother's religious views, but his long absence from England is likely to have entrenched the gulf between them. This was especially the case because it was Lord Chesterfield, through his letters, who acted as Francis's mentor through Europe. Chesterfield had sound advice on the culture and sights that Francis should take in. But he was also frank about the pleasures a young nobleman should expect in Francis's circumstances, and on the way he should treat the women he encountered:

> I have met with no one body absurd enough to suppose that you left England a spotless virgin, or to expect, if you had, that you would have returned such to it . . .

> If (as I suppose was the case) Mademoiselle Lany [leading dancer at the Paris Opera, and soon to be the mother of a child by Francis] prevailed with you to pass this winter at Paris, the cause was, at your age, a very justifiable one . . . Her situation and degree of character made your connection with her for a time not unbecoming. It is the duration of those connections that makes them disgraceful, when the influence of the lady is

supposed to be extended from the senses to the understanding and conduct of her friend.

Lord Chesterfield to Lord Huntingdon, 15 November 1750 and 25 November 1751. A. Francis Steuart (ed.), *Letters of Lord Chesterfield to Lord Huntingdon* (1923), pp. 31, 52.

Chesterfield made equally plain to Francis his dislike of religious zealotry, which he termed 'the source of a thousand ills to society, but of a thousand pleasures to the enthusiasts themselves'. It was hardly a definition with which Lady Huntingdon would have concurred.

Lady Huntingdon was no more successful in attracting her eldest daughter, Elizabeth, to evangelical religion. In 1749 the eighteen-year-old Elizabeth had a taste of the standards her mother had set for her; according to contemporary reports, Lady Huntingdon had removed her from her position at Court, when she found that it would involve her in Sunday card games. There followed a clash of wills, with Lady Huntingdon even attempting to prevent Elizabeth from reading standard works of English literature. Her life was a far cry from her brother's tour through the flesh-pots of Europe. But Elizabeth remained impervious, even when Whitefield attempted to convert her, praying in aid the story of a young woman who had made a death-bed conversion. There was only one way out, and in 1752 she married an Irish peer, Lord Rawdon, subsequently Earl of Moira. She told her brother:

I lived a life of duty with my Mother. I own it grew wearisome at length, and was a strong inducement to my marrying – my situation in Ireland is happy, extremely so, in separating us so far asunder. It leaves me governess of my own actions.

Lady Rawdon to Lord Huntingdon, 13 December 1752. Huntington Library MS HA10413.

Lady Huntingdon took comfort in the belief that Rawdon was a serious and religious man. She may have had some justification for this belief: a decade later, during a brief rapprochement between Lady Huntingdon and the Moravians, he accompanied her on an extended visit to their settlement in Bedford and appeared much moved during the services. (Maybe Rawdon was more godly than his wife: she had at least one affair during the course of her marriage.) Mother and daughter apparently never met again, and there was to be minimal further contact between them. Elizabeth seems to have been permanently alienated from her mother's version of Christianity.

It is surprising that Lady Huntingdon, despite the breach she had experienced with her own mother, should have misjudged her relationship with Elizabeth so badly. Possibly she was swayed by the high view she developed of the duties that children owed to their parents: back in 1749 she had shocked Howell Harris by taking the side of a father who had forbidden his daughter to continue contacts with the Methodists. Interestingly, Lady Huntingdon did have some links with Elizabeth's children. She met her two elder grandsons when they came to London for their education in the 1770s, and charmed them with gifts. In the following decade she attended a granddaugher's wedding – though the bride had to defend herself from suspicions of being a Methodist! And in the last year of Lady Huntingdon's life we find her writing that 'nothing can come up to the affection of Lord Rawdon my grandson for me'. That last comment suggests a woman who continued to crave family affection, and who was still capable of attracting it. It reminds us that there was a gentler aspect to her personality, alongside the dictatorial zeal on which we tend to concentrate.

With Lady Huntingdon's elder son, however – just as with Elizabeth – poor judgement seems to have damaged chances of improved relations. This time it was not missionary enthusiasm so much as architectural taste that caused the problem. In 1755 and 1756, in preparation for Francis's return from the Grand Tour, she supervised building work at Donnington Park. In part this consisted of necessary repairs to the main building, but Francis also needed a new gallery to house the paintings and sculptures he had acquired in the course of his travels. It was an enterprise that involved Lady Huntingdon in substantial work over an extended period. But her hope that Francis would approve of the outcome was bitterly disappointed. Her gothic replacement windows, and the total mismatch between the new work and the old, were condemned by Francis and everyone else who saw it. Horace Walpole, for example, was scathing about the 'two tawdry rooms like assembly rooms at Blackheath' that had been added by the Countess. Francis told his sister that the enterprise had left him two thousand pounds out of pocket, but that he would have paid five hundred more to put the house back as it was before.

These family preoccupations did not mean that Lady Huntingdon was cut off from developments within the Revival. From early in the decade, for example, she took a close interest in Whitefield's plans to raise funds for a new, larger Tabernacle in Moorfields. The rebuilt Tabernacle was eventually completed in 1755. The following year Whitefield conceived the idea of opening a second London chapel, this time in the West End. His chapel in Tottenham Court Road was opened that autumn. But it was not placed under Lady Huntingdon's legal protection, in her capacity as a peeress, despite Whitefield's having toyed with that idea for a time. The legal advice they received was to the effect that Lady Huntingdon's patronage could not be used in such circumstances. We shall look, in chapter 7, at the legal position governing places of worship in eighteenth-century England, and see how Lady Huntingdon was subsequently to go down the road that she had earlier been told was not open to her.

Despite the interest she took in such schemes, however, it is difficult to be sure how settled Lady Huntingdon was in her faith during these years. As we have seen, her attraction to the more mystical forms of religion lasted well into the 1750s. As late as 1754 she was the dedicatee of a volume of sermons by the mystically minded clergyman Thomas Hartley, who was to become one of the English champions of the views of Emanuel Swedenborg, a Swedish scientist who believed he was in direct contact with the angels. In her correspondence in this period there is often talk of the trouble and tribulation she was passing through. This could imply some sort of serious religious crisis, although the truth is probably more mundane. Evangelical religion lends itself to dramatic self-analysis, especially with those, like Lady Huntingdon, who are given to introspection. She wore her soul on her sleeve, and every day for her seems to have been a spiritual battlefield.

The 1750s saw several changes of home, however, and this may be a sign of her continuing uncertainty of direction. She gave up her Chelsea house some time in the early 1750s. Later she decided against settling more permanently at the family home in Ashby, in favour of a move to Clifton, near Bristol. The initial attraction of Clifton included the fact that it offered convenient access to Charles Wesley in Bristol. She and Charles were particularly close at this stage, feeding each other's hostility towards John Wesley, and making Whitefield anxious that he was being ousted from her favour. In 1755 she decided to move to a larger house in Clifton, and to use it to satisfy her earlier hankering after life in some kind of religious community. The background to this lay in Lady Huntingdon's links with a circle of women who were, for a while, to play an important part in her life. One of these was Ann Grinfield, who was serving as 'Bedchamber Woman' to the Royal Princesses (the same role that had been held briefly by Lady Huntingdon's daughter Elizabeth). Grinfield was a convert to Methodism who sought to use her official position to spread the faith – and who looked to Lady Huntingdon to supply her with guidance and arguments to use to this end. Lady Huntingdon thought this a marvellous opportunity to convert the Court, though she counselled Grinfield not to mention her name too much. That was no doubt wise advice, but it did not prevent Grinfield from making unguarded remarks about Lady Huntingdon's propensity to talk directly to God and the angels (shades, perhaps, of Swedenborg). Grinfield's excitable religious zeal did not go down well at Court, and when she left in 1755 it was generally believed she had been dismissed.

It was then that she went to live with Lady Huntingdon in Clifton. Lady Huntingdon had already begun her little community with two other women, Elizabeth Skrine and her stepdaughter Ann Barlow, who had had some previous experience of sharing together in an ordered life of reading and prayer. Lady Huntingdon described them as:

> . . . a sweet little family who live but to devote every hour more and more to the love and knowledge of the Lord Jesus. We had agreed upon this retreat, and taken a larger house among us for this purpose, and we all wish your prayers. To become the Lord's in body, soul, and spirit, is the one cry and desire of our hearts.

Lady Huntingdon to the Revd Risdon Darracott, quoted in J. Bennett, *The Star of the West* (London, 1813), pp. 169–70.

There was a sub-plot to all this, in the person of a former friend of Lady Huntingdon, Mrs Catherine Edwin. Mrs Edwin (once memorably described by Doddridge as wearing 'a furbelowd and pinckd Sack') was a Moravian sympathizer, who believed that her own, more restrained, presentation of her faith was likely to be more effective at Court than anything associated with Lady Huntingdon. She was not pleased at news of the Clifton community, which she saw as posing a direct threat to the Moravians' newly established congregation in Bristol. If such a challenge is what Lady Huntingdon had intended, however, she did not succeed. The Bristol Moravians proved so attractive to the other three women that they (and Mrs Edwin) eventually joined their congregation. So the lure of the Moravians meant that Lady Huntingdon's little community was short-lived. It is doubtful, however, whether it had really given her the peace she was seeking. She remained wracked by the old conflict between the desire to retire and attend to her own (spiritual) needs, and the sense that she was called to something more: she told Charles Wesley that what she most dreaded was to 'live for myself'.

Paradoxically – given the impact that Moravians had had upon her Clifton community – Lady Huntingdon was briefly to warm towards them herself as the 1750s progressed. A significant contributor to this was Howell Harris, who was emerging from his self-imposed isolation in Wales, and who was keen to restore harmonious relations between the Moravians and Methodism. Lady Huntingdon's softening of attitude led eventually to the short period of friendly relations between her and the Brethren in the early 1760s, which has already been mentioned. Another old rift that was healed in the 1750s was with Benjamin Ingham. Ingham appeared unexpectedly at the funeral of Lady Huntingdon's sister-in-law, Anne Hastings, in 1755. Afterwards Lady Huntingdon followed Ingham back to Yorkshire to see Margaret, and her contacts with the Inghams continued at least until Margaret's death in 1768.

The decade was also marked by an expansion in Lady Huntingdon's circle of clergy friends. She formed contacts with most of the big names among Anglican evangelicals during this period, and (with one important exception) they were all Calvinists in their theology. One of the first of these links was with James Hervey (1714–58), who had been one of John Wesley's pupils and a member of the Oxford Holy Club. Hervey's poor health, as well as his strong, principled objection to preaching outside the parochial system, meant that he spent most of his time quietly in his Northamptonshire parish. His contribution to the Revival was through his popular verse and prose writings. Hervey claimed that he avoided contentious Calvinist issues like predestination, but his works (in his lifetime and subsequently) became a focus for attack by John Wesley because they contained the Calvinist idea that Christ's righteousness was 'imputed' to sinners. Wesley feared that if men and women were treated *as if* they were righteous, they would lose the incentive to seek actual holiness.

The other clergy with whom Lady Huntingdon became associated in this period were more actively involved in mission. William Romaine (1714–95) came to her attention in 1755, when he was dismissed, because of his evangelical preaching, from the lectureship he held at the fashionable London church of St George's, Hanover Square. His name was formally added to the list of Lady Huntingdon's chaplains in 1761. Romaine, who subsequently became rector of St Anne's, Blackfriars, wrote a series of influential devotional works, and was one of the leading London evangelicals of his day. He was also one of the significant group of individuals who eventually parted company with Lady Huntingdon. Another prominent London evangelical was Martin Madan (1726–90), a former barrister. Lady Huntingdon appears to have used her influence to help Madan to be ordained, following his conversion, and for a period in the mid 1750s she was in close and frequent contact with him. Like Romaine, Madan became one of Lady Huntingdon's personal chaplains in 1761. Madan's principal occupation was as chaplain to the Lock Hospital, in London, which was an institution for fallen women. It was Madan's experience here that led eventually to his estrangement from his fellow evangelicals. He became convinced, from the women he met at the Lock, that an important incentive to prostitution would be removed if men were required to marry any women they seduced, *even if those men were married already*. This apparent support for polygamy caused evangelical outrage when Madan published his views in 1780.

Henry Venn (1725–97) was another of the young evangelical clergymen who entered Lady Huntingdon's circle in the 1750s. There is some evidence, indeed, that Lady Huntingdon was one of those who influenced Venn in the direction of evangelical beliefs in mankind's sinfulness and complete dependence on Christ for salvation. Venn was at that stage curate of Clapham – the church where his son John, who was to become a prominent member of the so-called 'Clapham Sect' of Anglican evangelicals, was later to be rector. The main phase of Venn's ministry, however, was as vicar of Huddersfield from 1759 until 1771, when his health compelled him to move to the country parish of Yelling in Huntingdonshire. The next recruit to Lady Huntingdon's circle was John Berridge (1716–93), a former Cambridge don, who had become vicar of Everton in Bedfordshire in 1755. Towards the end of the decade, Berridge passed through a conversion experience which had such an impact on his preaching that a revival broke out in his parish and the surrounding area. News of this reached the leaders of the Revival, some of whom (possibly including Lady Huntingdon herself) travelled out to Everton to see for themselves. John Wesley was particularly impressed:

> Mr Berridge appears to be one of the most simple as well as most sensible men of all whom it has pleased God to employ in reviving primitive Christianity . . . His word is with power; he speaks as plain and home as John Nelson [an early convert and lay preacher], but with all the propriety of Mr Romaine and tenderness of Mr Hervey.
>
> John Wesley to Lady Huntingdon, 10 March 1759. *Letters*, iv, 58.

The final significant addition to Lady Huntingdon's clergy friends in these years was John Fletcher (1729–85). Fletcher was a French-speaking Swiss, who had been in England since 1750, and ordained since 1757. His principal links were with John Wesley, and, unlike the other clergy mentioned, he was not a Calvinist. In 1760 he became vicar of Madeley in Shropshire, but he was later to play a key role in Lady Huntingdon's Connexion by agreeing to serve as the first president of her college at Trevecca.

The 1750s ended on a tragic note for Lady Huntingdon and her family. The year 1758 saw the death of her youngest son, Henry, at the age of eighteen. That left her daughter Selina as her one child still at home – and she in turn died only five years later. This raises the question whether either of these young people gave their mother grounds for thinking they had adopted her religious views. It was claimed after her death that she had said that none of her family 'besides herself and a cousin had the appearance of the fear of God' – though this can only be true if it referred to her Shirley relations, and not the Hastings. One of Lady Huntingdon's recent biographers finds it telling that no letters have been preserved from Henry or Selina giving any sign of evangelical sympathies. That could be significant, although it is of course dangerous in history to draw firm conclusions on the basis of what does *not* exist. Lady Huntingdon was certainly persuaded that Henry died in a state of grace. And the detailed accounts that Lady Huntingdon wrote of Selina's apparent death-bed conversion, though they may have gained in the telling, are unlikely to have been a total invention.

Another family bereavement occurred in 1760, and it was very different from those we have been looking at. This was the execution for murder of Lady Huntingdon's cousin, the 4th Earl Ferrers. In January 1760 Ferrers, who was on the brink of madness (if not actually over it), killed the steward who had been appointed receiver of his estate, following the Earl's estrangement from his wife. He was tried by his peers and convicted. Despite attempts by Lady Huntingdon and others to secure a reprieve (and visits by her to the condemned man), Ferrers was hanged at Tyburn in May. The conviction meant that part of the Earl's estates was escheated to the Crown, and this further complicated the long-running dispute, still not settled, over the family's inheritance from Lady Huntingdon's father. Nor, given that some people doubted the sanity of those who held evangelical beliefs, did the case help Lady Huntingdon's reputation. Six years after the execution, the affair was still the subject of (confused) gossip at Bath:

> We are now told concerning Lady Huntingdon, that her Son has taken out a Statute of Lunacy against her: that Madness is incident to the family: and that she is Sister to that Lord Ferrers, who was hanged at Tyburn not long since for wilfully killing his Man.
>
> John Penrose, *Letters from Bath, 1766–67*, ed. Brigitte Mitchell and Hubert Penrose, Gloucester: Alan Sutton, 1983, p. 60.

The 1750s cannot be regarded as a particularly satisfactory decade for Lady Huntingdon. At the end, as at the beginning, she was confused as to what she should be doing. Was she intended for a contemplative prayer life – perhaps augmented by purely personal acts of evangelism and benevolence? In such ways she could have made a real contribution to the religious life of her time – although there would probably not have been a book to write about it! But she seldom seemed convinced that this was all she could offer. There were two more strategic paths she might have taken. One would have been as a focus of unity within the Revival: an influence (using, if need be, the prestige of her rank) to calm frayed egos and to remind the leaders that they were not in the movement for their own gratification. The other would have been to use her social position more overtly to commend the faith, and to protect the movement's interests at local and national level.

The trouble was that by 1760 she had used up much of the moral capital needed to meet either of those objectives. She could not be the truly unifying force that she might have wished within the movement, because she allowed herself to become too closely associated with individuals. This made it hard for others to see her as dispassionate and unbiased. She was too much in the fray to rise effectively above it. This was a shame, because on occasions when she did manage to overcome differences – as in 1759, during fears of a French invasion, when she hosted a series of prayer meetings in which the Wesleys, Whitefield, and other prominent evangelicals took part – it could prove a rich and uniting experience (particularly, in this instance, for the Wesley brothers themselves).

Socially, too, she had damaged her potential influence through the enthusiasm (or eccentricity) with which she embraced her cause. As she recognized in the case of Ann Grinfield at Court, association with her could be counter-productive. If that were already true in the 1750s, it did not augur well for the decades to come. The Prince of Wales, who died back in 1751, may well have respected her and been influenced by her views. He is said to have rebuked a mocking remark about Lady Huntingdon with the words, 'When I am dying, I shall be happy to seize the skirt of Lady Huntingdon's mantle, to lift me up with her to Heaven.' If true, this is an impressive testimony. But what the anecdote also implies is that, even then, ridiculing Lady Huntingdon was assumed to be acceptable in Court circles.

The truth is that Lady Huntingdon caused mixed reactions in those who encountered her, so that it is difficult to generalize about how she was regarded. Here are two comments on her, delivered within 18 months of each other, the first by someone in broad sympathy with her religious position, and the other decidedly not:

[Lady Huntingdon delivers] a hotch-potch of opinions gleaned from everywhere without discretion, which, as she delivers them, encounter each other with repugnancies, to the amazement surely of the shrinking, to the admiration of the simple and the confusion of her own heart.

George Stonehouse to Charles Wesley, 2 April 1755. Meth. Arch. (Letters to Charles Wesley).

Let me beg you, my dear Lord, to say nothing to Lady Huntingdon ... that may produce the least coldness between you; for in that case, though she should be ever so much in the wrong, and you ever so much in the right, the public, generally in the wrong too, would take her part ... Her character is a very popular one, her enthusiasm has raised it with many people and has lowered it with none.

Lord Chesterfield to Lord Huntingdon, 9 October 1756. A. Francis Steuart, *Letters of Lord Chesterfield to Lord Huntingdon*, pp. 108, 109.

Whether Lady Huntingdon realized it or not, it seems likely that, by the end of the 1750s, the opportunities for her to use her influence outside the movement, or to offer wise counsel within it, were narrowing. In fact, she was poised to take the first steps in a new direction that would lead to a connexion of her own. Paradoxically, that may have weakened still further both her independence within the movement, and her chances of serious respect outside.

7

The 1760s: Opening Chapels and Recruiting Helpers

❧

Before the 1750s were over, Lady Huntingdon had found a new geographical focus for her evangelical activities. This was Brighton, then beginning to emerge as a fashionable resort. It is a pity – especially given the extensive documentation of so many aspects of her life – that we cannot be certain what first led her to the town, or what her original motives were in deciding to open a chapel. Various explanations have been preserved, however – some from an early date – and there may be some truth behind each of them. According to one account, it was her son Henry's final illness that first brought Lady Huntingdon to the restorative environment of Brighton. In another version, it was while in Brighton that Lady Huntingdon was overheard ministering to the physical and spiritual needs of a soldier's wife who had just given birth to twins – and was then prevailed upon to extend her care to a group of poor women who came together spontaneously to seek instruction from her. This is not implausible: direct ministry of this kind is something we know she engaged in.

Another anecdote involves Lady Huntingdon being accosted by a Brighton woman, previously unknown to her, who told her that she had dreamed, years earlier, of a person answering the Countess's current description, who was to come to the town and do much good. This story was recorded by Augustus Toplady, another of Lady Huntingdon's clerical associates, who claimed to have been told it by Lady Huntingdon herself, within 20 years of the supposed events. So, strange as it is, it may also have some substance. It is certainly feasible that Lady Huntingdon would have taken seriously accounts of revelations through dreams.

Whatever the truth of these stories, it was quite logical for Lady Huntingdon to make Brighton the next stage in her work. By the mid-eighteenth century Brighton's popularity as a fashionable place of resort had led to a significant growth in both residents and visitors. But its numbers of places of worship had not kept up with this expansion. So Lady Huntingdon could well have decided that it would be useful to fill that gap. Or she may have gone further and recognized that Brighton was well placed to be the focal point from which to undertake the evangelization of Sussex – an area of the country into which Wesley's followers had not yet penetrated very far. In 1759 Whitefield came down to preach in the open air at Brighton, and this could have had the wider purpose of testing the scope for a more permanent ministry in the town.

The alternative explanation is that Lady Huntingdon just stumbled by chance into the new sphere of work to which Brighton led her. Having come to Brighton for her son's sake, and started the ministry at differing levels of society to which she had become accustomed, she might then have recognized the value of purpose-built premises in which to hold meetings. Maybe her group of 'poor women' grew too large to be accommodated in any other way. Whatever the reason, she had a chapel built in 1761 alongside the house she had acquired in North Street, Brighton. Martin Madan conducted the opening service. In order to finance this enterprise, she borrowed money from one of her aristocratic sympathizers, Lady Gertrude Hotham, Lord Chesterfield's sister – eventually repaying her out of funds that had come to her from Lady Betty Hastings's will, more than 20 years before.

In opening a chapel Lady Huntingdon was not necessarily setting up as an alternative to the services provided by the Church of England. She could well argue that she was simply providing a meeting place for the religious society that had now formed – and that for more formal worship, including Holy Communion, her followers would be expected to attend the parish church. Nevertheless, the fact that Lady Huntingdon had established (and was expanding) a coterie of Anglican clergy meant that Anglican services were frequently on offer at her chapel. So the Brighton chapel, and the others that followed it, provided an alternative setting for the religious life of those who attended. The first steps had been taken towards the establishment of the Countess of Huntingdon's Connexion as a denomination of its own.

The legal basis upon which Lady Huntingdon opened her chapel was interesting. The general position established by the Toleration Act 1689, after the Glorious Revolution of the previous year, was that Dissent was still unlawful, save in certain clearly defined circumstances. The earlier penal laws, including the severe provisions against Dissenters passed under Charles II, remained in force. What the Toleration Act did was to exempt from those provisions such Dissenting ministers and places of worship that were duly authorized in accordance with the Act's provisions. Any place of worship which was not properly registered was not only unlawful, but missed out on the protection against popular disturbance that the Act gave to registered places. This meant that there were only two sorts of lawful religious premises: Anglican churches and chapels, and meeting-houses registered under the Act. The fact that there was supposedly no middle way posed a dilemma for the leaders of the Revival when they reached the stage of starting to build chapels. You could (at least in theory) only be lawful if you called yourself a Dissenter – something which many of them, with strong Anglican roots, were loath to do.

Wesley tried initially to get round this difficulty by arguing that the old penal provisions were irrelevant to a new movement like Methodism, which remained loyal to the Church of

England. Subsequently he found that it was possible to register a chapel under the Toleration Act without actually having to say that it was for use by Dissenters, and this was a device that some of his followers tried for a while. All the same, use of the Act still implied an unwelcome distancing from the Church of England. In Lady Huntingdon's case, however, there appeared to be a better way round the legal provisions – the entitlement (whether soundly based in law, or not) for members of the peerage to have a domestic chapel attached to their residence, and outside the jurisdiction of the bishop. Once such a chapel had been established, members of the public could be admitted to its services. The early chapels opened by Lady Huntingdon all had houses adjoining, so preserving the pretence that they were domestic in intention, whether or not the Countess was actually in residence. Sometimes the house in question would be let, but services still continued in the chapel. Nearly 20 years were to elapse after the opening of the Brighton chapel before a challenge was mounted to the doubtful legality of Lady Huntingdon's approach.

Whatever it was that Lady Huntingdon intended when she opened the Brighton chapel, it was not long before she extended her operations in the area. Within a year she reached an agreement with the owner of a house called Ote (or Oat) Hall at Wivelsfield, some eight miles north of Brighton. Lady Huntingdon rented the house, retaining parts of it for residential purposes (for herself and visiting ministers) while converting the main hall into a chapel. This was a significant development: not the provision of premises for a religious society already in existence, but the opening of premises designed to bring such a group into existence. Lady Huntingdon was taking the initiative in a way she had not done before. Sometimes the house was used for what sound like spiritual house-parties – perhaps a return to the model of a religious retreat that Lady Huntingdon hankered after so often – while at other times it was an active centre for mission in the area:

I discourse in the family here every day & publicly several times ... Not an hour passes [?uselessly] all the conversation is solid & weighty. Here is Sir Charles Hotham & 2 elderly ladies, all of one spirit.

Howell Harris at Ote Hall to [? Hannah Bowen or Mrs Harris], 1 June 1765. *Trevecka Letters*, No. 2603.

Such a time I scarce ever knew as we have had at Oat Hall. I met the society twice, and had spoken to them one by one for two Sundays before we had the sacrament; we were about one hundred communicants fed at the Lord's table ... Surely Oat Hall is a highly favoured place.

William Romaine to Lady Huntingdon, n.d. Quoted in A. H. New, *The Coronet and the Cross* (1857), p. 182.

Interestingly, in view of what we have seen about the legal position of chapels in the eighteenth century, Ote Hall was registered in 1762 under the Toleration Act – as a 'Presbyterian' meeting-house. We do not know whether this was Lady Huntingdon being cautious, or whether the registration was made without her agreement; a year later the registration was cancelled because 'Lady Huntingdon desires it should be done'. Ote Hall operated as a Connexional chapel in its own right, although the close proximity of Wivelsfield to Brighton meant that the two chapels were often treated as a unit for the purpose of arranging preaching supplies.

Sussex was the scene of considerable religious activity in the 1760s, and Lady Huntingdon seems to have been associated with a good deal of it – even though precise links are difficult to establish. In 1764 and 1765, for example, seven new independent chapels were registered in the county – three of them in the name of a man who was also actively involved in the Countess's chapels at Brighton and Ote Hall. And of the seven, at least four (as well as a number of other places in the county) received visits during the 1760s from preachers associated with Lady Huntingdon and based at Brighton.

Lady Huntingdon's experiences at Brighton clearly convinced her of the advantages of having premises of her own from which to operate. In 1765 she repeated the experiment in Bath, a town with which her own links went back more than 30 years. From remarks by one of her clerical associates, it seems that informal attempts had already been made at ministry in Bath, before the major step was taken of building a chapel and adjoining chapel-house in the fashionable Vineyards area of the town. The Bath chapel was not to be used in quite the same way as at Brighton, as the hub for evangelism in the surrounding area. But it seems to have been aimed, even more overtly, at fashionable society. Over the years, excited correspondents would tell of the aristocratic and other distinguished individuals seen attending the chapel services. This included some clergy, and on at least one occasion a bishop was spotted among the worshippers. For some people, no doubt, attendance at the Countess of Huntingdon's chapel was regarded as one of the curiosities to be experienced during the season at Bath.

The chapel itself seems consciously to have been designed with a fashionable appeal in mind. It was built on a much grander scale than her original chapel at Brighton, and must have seemed to some observers as deliberately provocative. Certainly Lady Huntingdon sensed open hostility to what she was planning, and this probably encouraged her that she was doing the right thing. While construction was still under way, she wrote, 'My chapel is above ground & I find I am heartily *wished to die* before it is finished.' Fortunately it is possible to see what the place was like, since it still exists. (It now serves as home to the Building of Bath Museum.) It is a rare example of a chapel surviving in the form in which Lady Huntingdon would have known it. It is elegant and imposing, decked out with gothic features that were no doubt meant to show that it was at the forefront of aesthetic taste. That noted arbiter of (particularly gothic) taste Horace Walpole was an early visitor, and claimed some influence over the interior design:

> They have boys and girls with charming voices that sing hymns in parts to Scottish ballad tunes ... The chapel is very neat, with true Gothic windows ... but I was glad to see that luxury is creeping in upon them before persecution ... At the upper end is a broad *haut-pas* of four steps, advancing in the middle; at each end of the broadest part are two of *my* eagles with red cushions for the parson and clerk. Behind them rise three more steps, in the midst of which is a third eagle for pulpit. Scarlet arm chairs to all three. On either hand a balcony for elect ladies. The rest of the congregation sit on forms ... Except for a few from curiosity, and *some honourable women*, the congregation was very mean.

Horace Walpole to John Chute, 10 October 1766. W. S. Lewis, *Horace Walpole's Miscellaneous Correspondence*, Newhaven and London: Yale University Press, 1973, p. 119.

This early reference to the quality of singing at the chapel is noteworthy, since high musical standards were obviously important in attracting refined worshippers. The signs are that standards were maintained. Some years after Walpole's visit, at a concert to inaugurate a new organ in one of Bath's Anglican churches, the combined choir consisted of choristers from Salisbury cathedral, voices from the local theatre – and singers from Lady Huntingdon's chapel!

We should not imagine, however, that aristocratic patronage told the whole story of the Bath chapel, even in Lady Huntingdon's day. The evidence is that the core membership of the congregation – on whom fell the hard graft of managing and maintaining the chapel – mainly consisted, as elsewhere in the Connexion, of small tradesmen and artisans. As Lady Huntingdon described the position, a year after the chapel opened, Sunday mornings were when 'the great of this world' usually attended; 'the evenings, the inhabitants chiefly'. It was also the case that, with the opening of the Bath chapel, Lady Huntingdon began to experience some of the daily pressures and problems that were to mark the rest of her life. She now had three pulpits to fill with preachers, and only the good will of her band of clerical friends on which to depend. And her priorities and theirs did not always agree. When the Bath chapel opened, for example, she had an argument with Romaine over whether it was better for him to attend the celebrations or (as he preferred) to continue serving the Brighton and Ote Hall congregations.

As well as service in her chapels, Lady Huntingdon looked to her clergy friends to take the message out by undertaking preaching tours, sometimes going with them herself. The year 1765, for example, saw her planning a trip to Derbyshire with Romaine and Venn, and a tour through Kent with Venn and Madan. Possibly it was on the latter occasion, or even earlier, that she conceived the idea of making Kent a further sphere of activity, with the emerging spa town of Tunbridge Wells as the centre. By 1768 she had bought a house in the Mount Ephraim area of the town, and established regular preaching. Subsequently she acquired a suitable nearby spot on which to build the chapel that Whitefield opened for her in 1769. This was one of his last public acts in England before he made his final visit to America, where he died the following year. Like the Brighton and Bath chapels, Tunbridge Wells was purpose-built for Lady Huntingdon, and at her expense. In this, and the fact that all three were in fashionable centres, they proved to be the exception, rather than the rule – despite what is popularly believed about her ministry and its direction. As we shall see, the majority of the chapels that bore her name during her lifetime were funded by other people, and were often converted from existing buildings. And many were in locations that were anything but fashionable.

The maintenance of services in her chapels, plus any other missionary activities (like preaching tours) that Lady Huntingdon wished to promote, demanded an extensive cadre of clergy on which she could call. With some important exceptions, especially Howell Harris, and the students from her college that we shall look at shortly, Lady Huntingdon was not generally attracted to lay preachers in the way Wesley was. But clergy were rarely free agents. The majority had parish commitments of their own, which they were reluctant to give up; assisting Lady Huntingdon generally meant finding curates to cover in their absence. (At least one, Henry Venn, preferred not to be away from home during his children's holidays.) So Lady Huntingdon was always on the lookout for new helpers, and her circle expanded considerably during the 1760s – so much so that by the late 1760s she could count on some 20 clergy willing to help her from time to time. They were a varied group of individuals, and it is interesting to look at some of them to see what sort of Anglican clergy were drawn into her sphere at this stage.

The most socially distinguished was one of Lady Huntingdon's own cousins, the 'Reverend and Honourable' Walter Shirley (1725–86). Walter was the brother of three Earl Ferrers, starting with the one who was hanged. He held a Shirley family living at Loughrea in Ireland, and according to some accounts kept a pack of hounds in Ireland, until his evangelical conversion through the influence of Henry Venn. It was probably the trauma of his brother's trial that brought him into closer contact with Lady Huntingdon, and from that time he gave periodic assistance to her work in England. After Whitefield's death in 1770, he succeeded him as one of her official chaplains. Shirley had no great love for his Irish parish, and he often talked of wanting to exchange it for one in England, where he would be able to give more help to Lady Huntingdon. But preferment did not come easily to evangelical clergy, even to those with aristocratic connections. Nor, as we shall see, did another plan to bring him to England work out. So the looked-for move never materialized.

Thomas Haweis (1734–1820), who entered Lady Huntingdon's circle in the early 1760s, was to play a major part in the

Connexion, both during her lifetime and after. Haweis had gone up to Oxford in 1755, already an evangelical, and after ordination in 1757 became curate to the evangelical vicar of the Oxford church of St Mary Magdalen. While he was at Oxford, he brought together a group of pious undergraduates that was reminiscent of Wesley's Holy Club. To the young James Woodforde (Parson Woodforde), who heard him speak in 1761, Haweis was already 'a famous Methodist', though Woodforde thought what he said was 'very stupid, low and bad stuff'. The following year episcopal and other hostility forced Haweis to give up his curacy, and he found temporary employment as Madan's assistant at the Lock Hospital. That in turn led to contacts with Lady Huntingdon, and occasional service at the Brighton chapel.

Then occurred an incident that was to blacken Haweis's reputation for many years, and which involved Lady Huntingdon as well. It related to the complicated law on church patronage, and to the fact that an advowson (the right to present a candidate to a church living) was a piece of valuable property. This was especially so when the present incumbent was elderly or infirm, when an early vacancy was expected. On the other hand, the rules were that an advowson could not be sold during an actual vacancy. In this case, Madan was approached in 1764 by a John Kimpton, who owned the advowson of the parish of All Saints, Aldwinkle, in Northamptonshire. Kimpton was in financial difficulties, but could not dispose of his advowson as the previous rector had recently died. So he was in a dilemma: appointing a young man to the living would reduce the value of his asset – but if he did nothing within a set period, he would, under church law, lose the right of presentation to the bishop. One solution would be to present someone who had given an undertaking that he would resign again, whenever Kimpton called upon him to do so. The problem was that this would have constituted the ecclesiastical offence of simony. Through Madan, Haweis was introduced to Kimpton, who, having explained his predicament, offered him the Aldwinkle living. It was about that conversation that a dispute started as to what exactly had been said. Kimpton claimed that Haweis had made a gentleman's agreement to 'stand in the gap' at Aldwinkle, with the implication that he would resign later; Haweis said he had made clear that he would take the parish 'out and out', or not at all.

On these few fateful words depended the whole issue, but it is impossible now (and it was probably impossible then) to determine who was telling the truth. The affair became a *cause célèbre*, once it became clear that Haweis would not resign, especially after Kimpton had been imprisoned for debt. Pamphlets were issued on both sides, and the controversy continued for several years. Haweis and Madan were accused of reneging on a moral obligation, and behaving heartlessly to a distressed individual; the reputation of Methodism suffered in consequence. Lady Huntingdon clearly doubted the Haweis and Madan version of the story, and tried unsuccessfully to persuade Haweis to resign and go to America. Finally, in 1768, in despair at the impact the dispute was having, she decided upon unilateral action. Without consultation with any of the parties involved, she stepped in and purchased the advowson herself – an action which rescued Kimpton, but appeared to confirm the guilt of Haweis and Madan. Madan made his feelings very clear:

> Your Ladyship acquaints me that you have sent £1000 for the purchase of the advowson of Aldwinkle. This step your Ladyship may have taken with the best intentions – but, under all the circumstances of the case, it is very evident to me that the necessary consequence of it will be an increase of reproach and injury to my friend Mr Haweis's character, and my own: and therefore I hope your Ladyship will do us the justice, upon all occasions, to declare that this step has been taken without our knowledge, consent, or approbation.

Madan to Lady Huntingdon, 3 March 1768. E2/1(7), CF.

The affair showed Lady Huntingdon's impetuosity, even though it is difficult to know what else might have been done to defuse the situation. It damaged her relations with Haweis and Madan for some time, and the memory of the affair survived in the popular imagination: a decade later it was still being satirized on the London stage. So far as Aldwinkle itself was concerned, Lady Huntingdon passed the advowson to Walter Shirley, on the assumption that he would succeed to the living if Haweis resigned or died – thereby achieving the former's desired move to England. In fact Haweis outlived Shirley by more than 30 years, and remained rector of Aldwinkle until his death.

A few years younger than Haweis, though possibly associated with him in his Oxford Holy Club, was a Welshman, Craddock Glascott (1743–1831). Glascott was serving as a curate in Berkshire when Lady Huntingdon invited him to join her; he did so once he was free of his curacy in 1767. Glascott's case was exceptional, in that he came to work for her full-time, rather than being supported by a parish stipend. The fact that she employed him like this is an interesting indication of the way her activities had expanded by the middle 1760s – especially as Glascott proposed joining her to serve only 'country congregations', rather than her chapels which he thought too grand for his abilities. In fact, he was soon involved in all aspects of her work, as well as acting as an occasional curate for some of her other clerical helpers, in order to free them up to serve her. So far as one can judge from letters, Glascott was one of the most moderate and agreeable of all Lady Huntingdon's associates. He remained an important figure in the Connexion for the rest of Lady Huntingdon's life, even after he had returned to parish ministry in the 1780s.

Rowland Hill (1744–1833) was a very near contemporary of Glascott, but his background, character and career were very different. Hill was the younger brother of Richard Hill, who later succeeded to the family baronetcy and who was to be a prominent evangelical controversialist and MP. Despite – or perhaps because of – having two sons (and a daughter) who had embraced evangelicalism, the Hill parents were hostile when the young Rowland launched himself into irregular preaching, while still a Cambridge undergraduate. Once Hill had been brought into her circle in 1767, therefore, Lady Huntingdon sought to fill the parental vacuum, and also, although without much immediate success, to reconcile his family to his new beliefs. 'He was as my own son', she wrote '– received into my house and preached in my pulpits.' Sadly for Lady Huntingdon, this surrogate son was to disappoint her as much as some of her own children. Hill remained in favour for some years, preaching initially as a layman for her, and for Whitefield and others, including at Doddridge's old meeting-house in Northampton. After much struggle, Hill eventually secured ordination as a deacon, though he never managed to be made a priest. He was another example, like Shirley, of the fact that, for evangelicals, good family connections were not sufficient to guarantee ecclesiastical success. For a while Hill appeared a rising star of the new generation of evangelical preachers, even though he had a humorous pulpit style that upset some of his colleagues and hearers. What appears eventually to have alienated him from Lady Huntingdon was her suspicion that he was operating in opposition to her Connexion's interests in some parts of the country. Her hostility to her former 'son' became such that she ordered in her will that he should never be allowed to preach in any of her chapels.

We should notice three other clergymen who assisted Lady Huntingdon a great deal in the 1760s, but who do not seem to have had much involvement with her thereafter. One of them, like Hill, was well connected. Joseph Townsend (1739–1816) was the son of a Wiltshire MP – a fact that occasionally gave respectability to his ministry, even though his father was hostile to the Revival. Townsend had been converted to evangelicalism through his sister Judith, who in turn had been converted by Madan and who subsequently married Thomas Haweis – a sign of what a close-knit world the Revival could be at this stage. Townsend became rector of Pewsey in 1764, and this brought him close enough to Bath for him to be able to assist there regularly. His name occurs prominently among Lady Huntingdon's helpers during the 1760s. He was later better known as a geologist and writer on medicine than as an evangelical. William Jesse (1739–1815) overlapped with Haweis at Oxford, and may have been part of his Holy Club. He and Haweis became associated with Lady Huntingdon at around the same time; during the 1760s he combined service for her with tenure of a parish in Yorkshire. Last of this group was Richard De Courcy (c. 1743–1803), who was one of the curates Shirley employed in Ireland to free him for work with Lady Huntingdon. De Courcy eventually followed Shirley to England, apparently at Lady Huntingdon's invitation. For a period in the late 1760s he preached for her, including undertaking an extensive preaching tour in Sussex, as well as at other places, such as Whitefield's London Tabernacle. After 1770, when he finally secured ordination as a priest, he settled into parish ministry in Shropshire, remaining on friendly terms with Lady Huntingdon despite no longer being actively involved in her work.

These, then, were some of the 20 or so ministerial helpers that Lady Huntingdon gathered around her during the 1760s. With all this interest in attracting preachers, did Lady Huntingdon give any thought to preaching herself? Though women's ministry was not a major issue in the Revival, it was not absent altogether. Whitefield supported the idea of women preaching when he discussed the issue with Howell Harris in the 1740s (Harris was opposed); John Wesley thought it might be right for women to do so in exceptional circumstances; and Lady Huntingdon, even before her conversion, expressed interest in a woman said to be preaching at a Quaker meeting-house. As we have seen, there are frequent examples of Lady Huntingdon speaking directly about her faith to individuals and small groups, and she professed herself satisfied that there was no scriptural barrier to women taking on this role. She seems, however, to have drawn a distinction between speaking in an essentially domestic context, and standing up to preach in the context of more formal worship. She probably feared, with some justification, that for her to lead public worship would expose her congregations to even greater risk of ridicule than association with her did anyway.

The fact that Lady Huntingdon felt she needed such a large cadre of clerical helpers shows how much her own perspective on the work had developed since she took the first fateful step of opening the Brighton chapel in 1761. This was mission on a qualitatively different scale from the days of house meetings in her drawing room and other forms of personal evangelism. Some of the expansion was forced on her by circumstances: for example, the Brighton congregation grew so much that an enlarged chapel had to erected on the original site in 1767. Maybe at last she had made the choice – or found it had been taken for her – between activity and retired contemplation. Some idea may be gained of the scale and complexity of her work, even in the 1760s, from the following letter written to her from Bath by a lay friend, John Lloyd. Lloyd was then a prominent member of the Bath congregation, and he continued active in the Connexion's affairs for the remainder of the Countess's life and afterwards. This letter is just one example among many that might be quoted:

Mr Powley left us last Monday. I reimbursed him his expenses in going & coming, which was £12.12.0 & presented him with 5 guineas. I hope this execution of your command is agreeable to your wishes. Last Thursday I received a letter from Mr Fletcher who is ready to come whenever a supply for Madely is furnished . . . I had construed [his silence] into an acquiescence to your proposal of his coming the first week in March . . . He tells me he wrote to your Ladyship some time ago to inform you of the necessity of having a substitute . . . This delay would have shut us up had not the Lord mercifully inclined the hearts of Messrs Shepherd, Townsend & [Charles] Wesley to assist us.

John Lloyd to Lady Huntingdon, 6 March 1768. F1/1415, CF.

(Powley was Matthew Powley, curate of Slaithwaite, Yorkshire, and subsequently vicar of Dewsbury; Shepherd was Edward Shepherd, a Bath clergyman who helped at the Bath chapel, and elsewhere in the Connexion, in the 1760s and 1770s.)

Despite all this activity, the relative scale of Lady Huntingdon's work should not be exaggerated, however. In 1767 Wesley estimated that there were some 24,000 members of his societies in Great Britain and Ireland. This is an impressive figure, given that it was less than 30 years since his movement first started, but it still represents only a tiny fragment of the ten million or so inhabitants of the British Isles at the time. And compared to Wesley, Lady Huntingdon was operating on a far smaller scale – perhaps barely a tenth of Wesley's numbers were involved in religious activities initiated through her. Nor can we be certain quite what Lady Huntingdon intended with all this activity – if, indeed, she had any clear idea herself. At this stage it is unlikely that she envisaged forming a separate denomination. If pressed, she would probably have argued that her congregations existed to augment the spiritual life of the Established Church, rather as the old Anglican religious societies had sought to do. Of course such arguments became difficult to sustain, as congregations came increasingly to cater for all the religious needs of their members.

We have been looking in this chapter at the way Lady Huntingdon's evangelistic work developed in the 1760s. We have deliberately left to one side the biggest step of all that she took in this decade, the founding of her training college at Trevecca. We shall look at that in chapter 9. But before we do so, we need to consider some other aspects of her life in this period, particularly her relations with others within the Revival.

8

The 1760s: Relations with Others in the Revival

❧❀❧

We noticed earlier how the start of the 1760s had witnessed a brief reconciliation with the Moravian Brethren. Lady Huntingdon visited their settlement at Fulneck in Yorkshire in 1760, and in 1761, accompanied by her son-in-law and others, she made a four-day visit to the Moravian settlement in Bedford. Her stay included attendance at church meetings and services, and it persuaded the Moravian minister at Bedford that a real bond had been forged between her and the Brethren:

> We were glad to hear and feel that their visit here has been a real Blessing . . . Lady Huntingdon said: I own before you that I have been formerly much prejudiced against the Brethren, but I knew them not . . . I assure you that not only everything of a prejudice is gone, but I love you most tenderly, and shall cultivate that connection while I live.
>
> Moravian Diary, Bedford, 13 March 1761. Bedford Record Office MO 342, p. 256.

In January 1762 Lady Huntingdon returned to Bedford for an even longer visit. But these auspicious beginnings did not last. By 1765, the year that she and the Moravians both opened chapels in Bath (itself a sign of incipient rivalry), there was renewed hostility on her side. The origins of this are unclear. Theology may have come into it, since she developed some fixed views on what she thought the Brethren believed. But it is also likely – as with so many of the quarrels that marked her later life – to have stemmed from jealousy, and a suspicion that others were conspiring against her interests. Howell Harris risked her anger on several occasions by trying to persuade her to be reconciled with them. Harris was a determined ecumenist (on the day that Lady Huntingdon's Bath chapel was opened, he also attended services at the Moravian chapel and at Bath Abbey), but he made no headway with Lady Huntingdon. She dismissed from her chapel one of its most stalwart supporters, a Mrs Leighton, because of her Moravian sympathies, and claimed to believe that the Moravians were 'Papists holding transubstantiation'. Harris told Lady Huntingdon that her attitude to the Moravians was a sign of inner spiritual failings.

Lady Huntingdon's relations with John Wesley during the 1760s were even more unpredictable than with the Moravians. In part this was evidence of the general sensitivity of relationships at the heart of the Revival. But it also showed what a volatile and unpredictable individual she could be.

An early test of her relations with Wesley was an incident that occurred in 1763, and which threatened both Wesley's personal authority and the general credibility of his movement. It was triggered by two members of Wesley's Foundry Society in London, George Bell, a former soldier who had gained a reputation for holiness and powerful extempore prayers, and Thomas Maxfield. Maxfield had been the first Methodist lay preacher, who had subsequently obtained Anglican ordination in order to serve as Wesley's chief assistant in London. Bell progressed from claiming that he had attained perfection and immortality, to predicting the end of the world. This, he said, would happen on 28 February of that year. Although Wesley publicly dissociated himself from Bell's prophecy, it caused considerable general alarm in the days leading up to 28 February – and criticism of Methodism afterwards. Maxfield withdrew from the Foundry, taking with him around a hundred members with an extreme belief in Christian Perfection. The whole incident appeared to show the danger of the doctrine. Lady Huntingdon played no direct part in the furore over Bell and Maxfield, and this was a cause of some resentment on Wesley's part: he felt himself unsupported by his Calvinist friends, whom he suspected of using the incident as ammunition against one of his key doctrines. His suspicions, and the fact that they were more than justified, are shown in the following extracts:

For a considerable time I have had it much upon my mind to write a few lines to your Ladyship; although I cannot learn that your Ladyship has ever enquired whether I was living or dead. By the mercy of God I am still alive . . . although without any help, even in the most trying times, from those of whom I might have expected it. Their voice seemed to be rather, *'Down with him, down with him, even to the ground'* I mean (for I use no ceremony or circumlocution) Mr Madan, Mr Haweis, Mr Berridge, and (I am sorry to say it) Mr Whitefield. Only Mr Romaine has shown a truly sympathising spirit.

John Wesley to Lady Huntingdon, 20 March 1763. Wesley, *Letters*, iv, 206.

Enclosed is poor Mr Wesley's letter. The contents of it, as far as I am concerned, surprised me; for no one has spoken more freely of what is now passing among the people than myself . . . I pity Mr John from my heart. His societies are in great confusion; and the point, which brought them into the wilderness of rant and madness, is still insisted on as much as ever.

William Romaine to Lady Huntingdon, 26 March 1763. Quoted in L. Tyerman, *The Life and Times of John Wesley*, 1880, ii, 463.

Very soon after these events, Lady Huntingdon was to be distracted by the death of her daughter Selina. It was an unexpected and devastating blow, and months later her evangelical friends were still trying to raise her from her grief. So far as we know John Wesley was not one of those who offered her sympathy and support. For whatever reason, relations between them remained cool for the rest of the year. Nor, at this stage, does Charles seem to have been in particularly close contact. In November 1763, if Howell Harris is to be believed, Lady Huntingdon described John Wesley 'as an Eel, no hold of him, and not come to the truth'. (She was in a particularly critical mood that day; she also commented that Madan, Berridge and Venn were impulsive, 'but must be born with'.) The following January John addressed her an extra-ordinary letter of complaint at what he saw as her preference for Calvinist clergy. He began (ominously) by judging it right to tell her 'just what is in my mind, without disguise or reserve':

> I was perfectly indifferent about it [accompanying his brother to Lady Huntingdon's chapel in Brighton], being in no want of employment. It was therefore little concern to me that Messrs Whitefield, Madan, Romaine, Berridge, Haweis were sent for over and over, & as much notice taken of my Brother and me, as of a couple of Postillions. It only confirmed me in the judge-ment I had formed for many years [that] I am too rough a preacher for tender ears . . .
>
> . . . I am grieved for your Ladyship. This is no mark of Catholic spirit, but of great narrowness of spirit.
>
> John Wesley to Lady Huntingdon, 8 January 1764. E4/3(1), CF.

The rest of 1764 proved, however, to be a better year for their relations. Wesley had a positive meeting with Lady Huntingdon, some time after this letter, and in the light of it took the initia-tive in April of writing to some 30 or more evangelical clergy. Lady Huntingdon and another evangelically minded peer, Lord Dartmouth, also received copies. Wesley's intention, he explained, was not that everyone should be in absolute agreement either on doctrines or on how far they should stick to church rules on preaching within the parish system. That, he thought, would be impossible. What he proposed was a more modest commitment to mutual support and respect, and a resolution not to speak disrespectfully of one another. Lady Huntingdon was clearly in an accommodating mood, and sent an encouraging response – though she was one of only a handful of recipients of Wesley's letter who replied at all. Wesley proposed a general meeting of evangelical clergy, to be held following his annual conference in Bristol that August. Lady Huntingdon's association with this, said Wesley, 'might be of excellent service in confirming any kind and friendly disposition' that might emerge. Such a meeting did take place, although under her auspices, as much as his, at a large house she had recently taken in Bristol. A reasonable number of ministers attended, and Howell Harris thought it a great success. But though doctrinal issues were successfully avoided, the meeting stuck on the Wesleyans' refusal to keep preachers out of parishes served by evangelical clergy. (Lady Huntingdon was probably torn on this issue. Most of the clergy were fellow Calvinists, but as she was now sponsoring irregular preaching herself, she might well have had some sympathy with Wesley's position.)

So, for the moment, relations between Wesley and Lady Huntingdon looked promising. By the autumn of the following year, 1765, however, they had soured, so far as she was concerned. Why is unclear. Howell Harris, attempting to act the peacemaker, was puzzled by her hostility, trying unsuccessfully to persuade her that Wesley was the same man then that he had been the year before. But another year on, and we find yet another change of attitude, with Lady Huntingdon making a fresh attempt to improve harmony between herself, the Wesleys, and George Whitefield. The initiative took John Wesley by surprise, but he clearly had sufficient regard for her position within the Revival, that he altered his planned itinerary and made an unscheduled visit to London:

It was at the earnest request of [Lady Huntingdon] whose heart God has turned again, without any expectation of mine, that I came hither so suddenly: and if no other good result from it but our firm union with Mr Whitefield, it is an abundant recompense for my labour. My brother and I conferred with him every day.

John Wesley's *Journal* for 17 August 1766. Wesley, *Works*, xxii, 57.

In practical terms, the meeting led to Wesley preaching at the Bath chapel, later in the month. Wesley gave the impression in his *Journal* that he was indifferent whether he was asked to preach there again, or not. But he did offer to do so, and that offer was well received by Lady Huntingdon, who proposed that the four should meet up regularly 'to communicate our observations upon the general state of the work'. (Rather engagingly, she suggested such meetings would help guide *her*, as well as being of general benefit.) It is surprising she was in so benign a mood, given the report that was circulating – apparently believed by Charles Wesley, and already conveyed back to Lady Huntingdon by a third party – that the purpose of the August meeting had been to hand control of her chapels to Whitefield and the Wesleys. In other circumstances such a rumour might well have triggered Lady Huntingdon's paranoia, but this time she seems to have weathered it, and relations remained cordial. The following year, when the Bath chapel was being refitted, she proposed involving the Wesleys, Whitefield and Harris in the reopening ceremonies, in an act that would serve as a 'dedication of our remaining days'. With the hindsight of history, that comment has some poignancy, given the divisions that were soon to split the Revival, and the substantial work that lay ahead for most of them. Only Whitefield, as it turned out, was near the end of his life – and he was the only one of the four with whom Lady Huntingdon did not subsequently fall out.

9

Trevecca College

❧

In March 1768 an extraordinary event occurred at Oxford. Six undergraduates were expelled from the university for (as one London newspaper put it) 'having too much religion'. The six were all from the same college, St Edmund Hall, where the religious sympathies of the Principal, Dr Dixon, had led to the admission of a number of evangelical students. This did not please the Hall's vice-principal, John Higson, who was hostile to Methodism. Early in 1768 he made a formal complaint to the Vice-Chancellor about seven undergraduates (one of whom was to leave Oxford of his own accord). The remaining six appeared before the university authorities, charged with 'holding Methodistical tenets, and taking upon them to pray, read, and expound the Scriptures, and singing hymns in private houses'. A further factor in the case of some of the students was their social origins, and their alleged deficiency in Greek and Latin. Despite Dixon's evidence as to the students' conduct and Anglican loyalties – and support for the students from some other college heads – the judgement went against them.

The events caused considerable public interest, and pamphlets were published for and against the University's actions. The concern was not only over the justice of the case, but focused particularly on the Calvinist theology held by the students. The students had effectively been judged disloyal to the Church of England in professing Calvinist beliefs. The students' defenders, on the other hand, argued that Calvinism had been part of the core doctrines of the Church of England ever since the Reformation. It is interesting that whatever Wesley may have felt about the treatment of the individual students, he was pleased that the University's defenders had, in effect, 'cleared' the Church of England of Calvinism. The events of 1768 were thus the prelude to the much wider controversy about these issues that, as we shall see in chapter 12, was to split the Revival in the early 1770s.

Equally significant for our purposes was the fact that Lady Huntingdon was widely believed to have had links with the six students, or even to have funded them at Oxford. The events coincided with the climax of the Haweis/Aldwinkle scandal, so she had a controversial public profile already. Hence some people saw the affair, and her alleged involvement in it, as evidence of an evangelical plot to infiltrate the University and the Church. One commentator described St Edmund Hall as 'the place where a certain person sends all those who have a mind to skulk into orders'. Some of the students certainly had had links with other evangelical leaders, such as Haweis and Fletcher, and one of them had been tutored by John Newton. It is more difficult to decide, however, whether Lady Huntingdon herself had had any direct contact with them. We do know that she had been in correspondence with James Stillingfleet, the Oxford don who convened the house group at which the scandalous hymn-singing took place – and that she sent money to the tradesman who owned the house. We know also that she favoured students going to St Edmund Hall. It seems in fact to have been the news that Lady Huntingdon had recommended an evangelical to the Hall that had prompted Higson to make his complaint in the first place. And in May 1768, some months after the expulsions had taken place, there was more talk of her putting forward candidates to them.

If Lady Huntingdon had indeed encouraged or assisted the men to go to university, she would not have been alone among evangelicals in doing so. In 1767, for example, George Burnett, vicar of Elland in Yorkshire, founded the Elland Clerical Society, part of whose purpose was to assist evangelical ordinands to secure a university education. (In the early years this meant directing them to Cambridge, where the Society knew university teachers who shared their beliefs.) Against all this, however, it has to be said that Lady Huntingdon's correspondence with some of the expelled students does not suggest that they had been in earlier contact. And she herself vehemently denied having funded them:

> With the foul invectives of common newspapers I have nothing to do, neither am I accountable for the impudent falsehood of those who have maliciously asserted that I have inveigled six ignorant young men from their trades in the country, and maintained them at the University. All these, and many other absurd and ridiculous accusations . . . are utterly false.
>
> Letter of Lady Huntingdon (no date or recipient given). Quoted in *Life & Times of the Countess of Huntingdon*, i, 426.

More important than the role which Lady Huntingdon may or may not have played was the implication of the case for evangelicals hoping to be ordained into the Church of England. If evangelicals were under threat at the universities, then the prospect of securing more evangelical clergy would be seriously weakened. This was because a university education was the normal route to ordination in the Church of England. There were other worrying signs, also, so far as attitudes to evangelicals were concerned. In the same month as the expulsions, the Anglican Society for Promoting Christian Knowledge resolved to 'accept of no recommendation for persons to go abroad as missionaries, but such as have had a literary education, and have been bred up with a design to dedicate themselves to the ministry' – a clear sign of hostility to ordinands who were not university graduates, or who came from lowlier ranks in society.

What all this must surely have done was confirm for Lady

Huntingdon the rightness of a step she had been planning for some years, and which was now about to come to fruition. This was the founding of her own college for would-be ministers. The object, however, was to offer not just an alternative education to that provided by the universities, but a specific training in the skills that future ministers would need.

The idea of putting potential ministers through a dedicated course of training sounds fairly obvious to us today. This was not so in the eighteenth century. Most of the men ordained into the Church of England would have been at Oxford or Cambridge, and received a classical education. They were likely to have read some theological works along the way, but their course would not have contained anything expressly designed to prepare them for parish ministry. It was not until the second decade of the nineteenth century that the first college was established for non-graduate ordinands – and some time later again before provision was made to give graduates professional ministerial training. The same was the case for those ordained as Dissenters. The Dissenting Academies provided the equivalent of a university education, for students unwilling to make the subscription to the Church of England that was required of those who attended Oxford or Cambridge. The Academies' standards were often high. But their students were not exclusively ministerial candidates, and those destined for ordination rarely received specific ministerial preparation.

The general assumption was that, provided a man had an adequate general education, any necessary ministerial skills could be picked up on the job. Some evangelicals thought that this was not only sufficient, but right. If God had called a person to ministry, he would surely also provide him with the necessary skills: offering training somehow implied that one could improve upon the work of the Holy Spirit. John Berridge made this point forcefully to Lady Huntingdon while she was planning her college:

Are we commanded to make labourers, or to 'pray the Lord to send labourers'? Will not Jesus choose and teach and send forth his ministering servants now as he did the disciples aforetime? . . . We read of a school of prophets in Scripture, but we do not read that it was God's appointment.

Berridge to Lady Huntingdon, quoted in *Life & Times of the Countess of Huntingdon*, ii, 92.

Nevertheless, the idea of special training occurred to a number of the Revival's leaders. In the 1740s Wesley contemplated providing training for his lay preachers; in 1760 it was suggested to him that Methodism needed a college as a source of travelling preachers. The idea also occurred to some Dissenters. In the 1750s an academy was established at Heckmondwike in Yorkshire for training evangelical ministers; around the same time there were plans for a specifically evangelical academy in London. Lady Huntingdon may well have given some financial support to the latter, as she did to Doddridge's academy at Northampton, where again there was a conscious effort to nurture evangelically minded ministerial candidates. Most significantly (for our purposes), Howell Harris claimed to have had the vision of a 'School of the Prophets' (in that favoured phrase) in 1740, and that the idea 'had ever since abode in my heart in prayer'. By 1761 he was talking of an 'Academy for Preachers', which he thought might be linked to his settlement at Trevecka in South Wales. Once he had resumed contacts with Lady Huntingdon in 1763, he began to interest her in the idea, and in the following year tried to persuade John Fletcher to lead such an institution. The seed quickly took root in Lady Huntingdon's mind, as a way of meeting the requests for evangelical curates that were often put to her. In June 1764 she told Charles Wesley, 'I wish we had *a nursery* for these out of your lay preachers.' Over the coming year Lady Huntingdon took the first steps towards turning that aspiration into a reality.

The building chosen for the college was a farmhouse in

Trevecka in South Wales, Howell Harris's home village, and the location since the early 1750s of his 'Settlement' of craftsmen and artisans. The choice of Trevecka is a sign of how closely Harris was involved in the planning. It also showed a shrewd appreciation by Lady Huntingdon of the value of having Harris and his workmen close by, both during the conversion work, and after the college had opened. A further factor was doubtless the belief that a remote Welsh village would expose the students to fewer temptations and distractions than an urban setting. This was a wise precaution, since events over the next two decades showed that the students were not all angels, when it came either to application to study or relations with women.

The house was leased by Harris from his brother, and sublet to Lady Huntingdon for a term of 20 years. Its adaptation involved the creation of a chapel, and the provision of rooms for the students and accommodation for Lady Huntingdon and the college principal. The work dragged on because Lady Huntingdon was not on hand to take day-to-day decisions. Her on-site representative was Mrs Leighton from Bath, now restored to favour, but nothing of significance could be done without Lady Huntingdon's authority. Thus she had to be consulted by letter on such varied matters as the decoration of the chapel, and whether brewing equipment should be acquired as a cheaper alternative to buying beer for the students. The opening date was put back several times, to August 1768, and even then work on the chapel was only completed on the night before the opening. Harris had employed 24 of his men on the project, billing Lady Huntingdon £450 for labour alone.

In parallel with work on the building went a search for staff to teach, and students to learn. The first man Lady Huntingdon approached as tutor, towards the end of 1765, was Francis Okely (1719–94). Okely was a Cambridge graduate and a friend of Wesley, who had been ordained by the Moravians, but later failed in his attempt to be ordained into the Church of England. By the mid 1760s he was actively associated again with the Moravians, so he was a strange choice for Lady Huntingdon's college. Okely took the offer seriously – while seeking to satisfy himself on such practical considerations as whether the tutor's quarters would be furnished. Eventually, however, he pleaded his own inadequacy for the challenge that the college presented:

> I think the Scheme is admirable, but the Execution is the Difficulty. This none would be sufficient for, without a very extraordinary Aid. There are Schools and Academies enough, both on the Establishment, and in the dissenting Way, but a School of the Prophets, that's the Thing.
>
> Okely to Howell Harris, 10 April (1766). Roberts, *Selected Trevecka Letters*, ii, 102.

Instead of a Moravian sympathizer, Lady Huntingdon settled on a Wesleyan one, John Fletcher. In November 1767 Fletcher informed her that he would take on the college presidency 'so far as my present calling and poor abilities will allow'. By 'present calling' Fletcher meant his parish of Madely, which he retained, along with his other commitments within the Revival. So it was clear to him and to Lady Huntingdon that other teaching help would be needed. Their first idea was a 17-year-old former pupil of Wesley's school at Kingswood, called Easterbrook – the thought being that he would combine teaching and study alongside the other students. Easterbrook's youth made this a strange choice, although the principle of a senior student, combining teaching and study, was one to which Lady Huntingdon was to return: at various stages in the college's life the students were left to their own devices, under the guidance of one of their own number. But a moral lapse of some kind removed Easterbrook from the scene, before the college had even opened. Lady Huntingdon was forced to settle for the moment on a former teacher, John Williams, a Harris convert, who was engaged to teach basic Welsh and English grammar and some Latin.

Finding students of a good standard proved more difficult than Lady Huntingdon may have expected. This was probably a sign that most well-qualified candidates, even if they had heard of Trevecca, doubted whether it could offer the equivalent kudos and academic grounding of time spent at one of the universities. This was despite Lady Huntingdon's attempt to give Trevecca something of the aura of a university – for example, by the use of academic gowns, and the distinctive title 'college', rather than 'academy'. Nevertheless, Lady Huntingdon's clergy friends worked hard to find promising young men. By the end of 1767, when it was hoped to open the following spring, seven had been identified. One of these had been suggested to John Fletcher in a dream:

> In my sleep [I] was much taken up with the remembrance of one of my young colliers, who told me some months ago, that for four years he had been inwardly persuaded he should be called to speak for God. I looked upon the unusual impression of my dream as a call to speak to the young man ... His name is James Glazebrook, collier and getter of iron-stone. He is now twenty-three – by look nineteen; he has been awakened seven years.
>
> Fletcher to Lady Huntingdon, 24 November 1767. Quoted in *Life & Times of the Countess of Huntingdon*, ii, 81.

Only two of the expelled Oxford students accepted Lady Huntingdon's invitation to switch to Trevecca. This was a further sign of the reserve with which the new institution was regarded, even by devout evangelicals, because going to Trevecca offered no certainty of a ministerial career at the other end. If, as the St Edmund Hall expulsions had implied, getting to Oxford was no guarantee that an evangelical would be ordained, what hope was there for one from South Wales? Nevertheless, two were better than none, and together with a few more who were recruited by the time the college eventually opened in August 1768, this brought the initial number of students to around a dozen.

The other vital preparatory element was deciding what the students should be taught. This was left surprisingly late. At the end of 1767 Lady Huntingdon asked Fletcher for ideas about the books they would need – to which Fletcher replied quite reasonably that a 'plan of study' was needed before they could talk about equipping the library. Fletcher's suggestions for a curriculum show the underlying purpose of the college: general academic grounding, in order to bring the students up to a basic educational level, and then concentration on the specific knowledge and skills needed in evangelism. So far as the latter were concerned, Fletcher's suggestions for reading included books on pronunciation, metaphors and preaching, and Johnson's *Dictionary*. Only the more gifted students would be trained like traditional clergymen and do some Latin and Greek:

> Grammar, Rhetoric, with Ecclesiastical History, and a little Natural Philosophy [i.e., science], and Geography, with a great deal of practical divinity, will be sufficient for those who do not care to dive into languages.

> Fletcher to Lady Huntingdon, 3 January 1768. Quoted in *Life & Times of the Countess of Huntingdon*, ii, 85.

Despite Fletcher's efforts, John Wesley was doubtful how the college would turn out. 'Did you ever see anything more queer than their plan of institution?' he asked his brother in May 1768, adding (perhaps superfluously), 'Pray who penned it, man or woman?' He may well have doubted how someone of Lady Huntingdon's volatile personality would cope with the tutelage of a college of raw young men – since it was pretty certain she would not take a back seat, and leave the teaching staff to get on with it. He may also have feared the implications for his own work of the preachers produced by the college. Would they complement his work, or threaten it? Would they give Lady Huntingdon a competitive advantage, so far as leadership of the Revival was concerned?

After some four years of thinking and planning, the college was formally opened by George Whitefield on 24 August 1768, Lady Huntingdon's sixty-first birthday. Lady Huntingdon had arrived in some state, a few weeks earlier, accompanied by four ladies, the schoolmaster, a housekeeper, and two maids. John Wesley had told her that he might attend, but did not – although he was present at Trevecca to celebrate the first anniversary of the opening in 1769. The anniversary was observed as a special occasion for some years, not only at Trevecca, but at some of Lady Huntingdon's major chapels as well. This is a sign of the significant role that the college came to play in the life of the wider Connexion.

We shall look in a later chapter at how the college operated during the 23 years that it was located at Trevecka, and at some of the problems it experienced. But it is important at this stage to note a key development that occurred within a few weeks of the opening. This was the decision to allow – or maybe to *require* – the students to test out their skills with practical preaching in the vicinity of the college. As early as October 1768 the students started making preaching excursions into the neighbourhood, and the pattern was subsequently established of students preaching at locations up to a dozen or more miles from college. One example of this was Brecon, to which the students were invited by local people as soon as the college opened. The contact led to the formation of a congregation, and to the opening of a chapel later in 1769. In parallel with this outreach, the services in the college chapel were open to the public, so developing further the college's direct role in mission to the area. Brecon appears to have been the first place at which students stayed away overnight, and this marked an important further development in the way they were used. Before long a pattern of weekend preaching tours emerged, with selected students leaving on a Friday or Saturday and returning on the Monday.

As early as April 1769 Lady Huntingdon had thought of going a stage further again, by using some of the students in Bath (although not at her fashionable main chapel). Fletcher persuaded her to delay such a step until he had had a further opportunity to assess their abilities. Before the end of the year, however, Lady Huntingdon was sending students on extended preaching tours that took them right away from the college's home area. These might go on for a month or two, before the students returned to college. For example, Glazebrook was sent to the West Country with another student, Henry Mead. They were in Bridgewater in early January 1770, and returned to college via Herefordshire by mid February. The letter they sent to Lady Huntingdon, after their return, gives a flavour of the freedom (within limits) that students were allowed to follow up evangelistic opportunities as they arose:

... some time ago Glazebrook was preaching at a place called Long-town [Herefordshire], at which time he was importuned by one present to go to Ross ... Afterwards we received a letter from Mr Miller, a mercer of Ross, who being a Dissenter promised to get the use of their meeting. And as it was a new place, we thought it prudent to go ... two together ... But Satan was arrived there before us, for the Dissenters [decided] ... not to let us preach in their meeting ... But the above mentioned gentleman came to us at the Kings Arms Inn and asked the landlord the loan of his bowling green, which he readily granted together with his ballroom. The landlord of the inn behaved very civil to us, and more so, I believe, upon your Ladyship's account. Glazebrook preached in the bowling green to several hundred auditors: many of the higher rank were present, among which were the minister of the church ... [The minister subsequently denounces them as 'vagabonds' in his afternoon sermon, but this has the opposite of the desired effect, for] at 5 o'clock in evening, near if not more than a thousand assembled themselves together in the ballroom and yard, belonging to the inn, and Mead preached to them concerning the Publican and the Pharisee.

There was much entreaty made for our coming again . . . but as the journey must be accompanied with much expense, and loss of time for study, we thought it not prudent (though we have once done it) to engage again without acquainting your Ladyship with it.

Mead and Glazebrook to Lady Huntingdon, 15 February 1770. F1/87, CF.

By the early summer of 1770 Glazebrook was on the road again, this time in Brighton and the surrounding area, in company with a different student, William Aldridge.

The college had initially been conceived as a means of boosting the supply of evangelical clergy. As we shall see, it had only mixed success in this objective. But it made a rapid and significant contribution to Lady Huntingdon's supply of ministers, because she treated it as though its primary purpose was to provide her with a team of travelling preachers. The measure of its success – in her eyes, at least – was not so much the quality of its teaching and training, as its ability to meet her demands for preachers. Once the college had got into its stride, it was providing her with upwards of a dozen additional preachers a year – although this sometimes meant that the college itself was left with only a handful of students actually studying.

Students quickly became a key part of the Connexion's ministry, sometimes spending years on end away from college, either serving preaching circuits ('rounds' as they were called in the Connexion) or staying in a single location. This is why the founding of the college was such a significant step. It meant that from the start of the 1770s Lady Huntingdon acquired the manpower resources she had previously lacked, and her Connexion could begin a process of rapid expansion. Without the college, it is doubtful whether there would have been a Connexion in anything like the form it subsequently acquired. In the next chapter we shall see how this expanding Connexion operated on the ground.

10

How the Connexion Spread and Operated

ᗡᕼᔕ

The letter from Mead and Glazebrook quoted at the end of the previous chapter (pp. 97–8) is particularly interesting, as it shows in a number of ways how the Connexion operated, and the reactions it aroused:

- The students were invited to Ross by a resident of the town who was already sympathetic to evangelical preaching;
- although that person happened in this case to be a Dissenter, this was no guarantee that the local Dissenting congregation would welcome evangelical preachers;
- the local Anglican clergyman monitored what was happening, and immediately preached against the students;
- the students preached both out of doors (even in February) and indoors, depending on the premises available;
- large numbers of people turned out to hear them;
- association with Lady Huntingdon appeared to add some cachet to the students;
- when the students left, there was a possibility that a permanent congregation might be formed;
- it was within the students' discretion to respond to the original invitation, but they needed Lady Huntingdon's authority before making any future commitments.

There are many examples in the 1770s and 1780s of the Connexion's students or ministers entering an area, and then receiving invitations to neighbouring towns or villages. Such invitations were very helpful because they meant there was someone on the spot who knew about possible preaching venues, and who could provide accommodation for the preacher and attempt some form of advance publicity. Where there was a chance of a permanent congregation forming, they would be the natural people to try to organize things.

The religious background of these local contacts could vary considerably. They might have been influenced by the Revival already – because of course the Revival had been generating travelling preachers (Wesleyan and other) in different parts of the country for some 30 years before Lady Huntingdon became actively involved. Or they might be Dissenters or Anglicans who found their current services too dull or too unorthodox for their taste. As such they may have looked back nostalgically to the Puritanism of the seventeenth century, and hoped that the Revival would return the churches to what they believed were true Reformation beliefs. Or the people who issued invitations might simply have been individuals who took their religion seriously, and hoped that the visiting preachers would help their own spiritual development and that of their neighbours. This did not necessarily mean that they were looking to leave their existing denominations and move elsewhere. We should not suppose that all who welcomed the Connexion's preachers wanted to start new congregations.

A similarly broad spread of religious backgrounds could often be found among those who came to hear Lady Huntingdon's preachers – together with some individuals who were not currently involved in any sort of religious activity. Of course the Connexion, like other evangelical groups, liked to think they were bringing the gospel to lost souls who had never heard it before. And sometimes they were. But in practice a lot of the Revival's efforts were spent trying to attract religiously minded individuals away from one group to another. What was sometimes called 'sheep-stealing' – members of one congregation being poached by another – was a constant anxiety. Poor-quality sermons, or a period without a preacher at all, would make a congregation particularly vulnerable. 'Send us a better preacher,' local leaders would sometimes write to Lady Huntingdon – warning her that otherwise sections of the congregation would be seduced away to the Wesleyans, or the Baptists, or whoever it was that was currently providing the best preaching in town.

If members of congregations could be found from across the religious spectrum, their social origins tended to be more uniform. The majority of the Connexion's congregations seem to have been made up of small tradesmen and labourers. The gentry, and people with significant financial means, were much less in evidence. Nevertheless, most members of congregations were literate, judging from the multiple signatures that often appeared on the letters they sent to Lady Huntingdon. They were able to find, from within their ranks, intelligent individuals who were able to organize their affairs. And they do not seem to have felt that their ministry was confined to people of their own social group. They saw their mission as being to the whole community in which they lived.

We should not be too dismissive of those – like the Dissenters at Ross, and many Anglican clergy across the country – who opposed the students' preaching. Of course local church leaders may have feared competition, and the potential loss of adherents and income. And there may also have been a feeling that such informal and unauthorized preaching challenged local authority and threatened the fabric of society – especially if sermons appeared critical of existing clergy and ministers. But as well as this there were respectable – and disinterested – reasons for fearing the moral and emotional impact of dramatic evangelical preaching, particularly on vulnerable individuals. This legitimate fear was heightened when the message came from Calvinists who stressed that faith mattered more than conduct, and when it was delivered by young men who had more obvious zeal than education or life experience.

Violence, of course, was a different matter. There was never a justification for the vicious treatment that the mobs handed out to some of the Connexion's preachers – as they did at times to Wesleyan and other evangelical preachers. So far as the Connexion was concerned, this happened chiefly in the early 1770s, at the time when its work was expanding quickly – which suggests that it was the novelty factor that most raised popular fear and antagonism. Occasionally attacks were directed at the Connexion preachers taking services indoors, in chapels or meeting-houses, but it was open-air preaching that was most vulnerable to mob violence. Sometimes mobs would physically drive a preacher out of the town. At other times they pelted preachers with eggs, or subjected them to noisy interruptions or vandalism. Burning preachers in effigy was another dramatic, if harmless, way of expressing hostility. Some such acts may have taken place spontaneously, but there were many allegations that opposition, including violent opposition, had been encouraged and orchestrated by influential local people. It was most frequently the clergy who were thought to be behind the various forms of resistance that the Connexion encountered. It was, after all, their influence in the community that was most threatened by evangelical preaching. The gentry were also implicated on occasions. Sometimes mayors and magistrates showed themselves sympathetic to the Connexion's opponents, but there were also occasions where they defended the Connexion's right not to be subjected to violence.

It was because the Connexion responded so readily to local invitations that its growth often appeared spontaneous and unplanned. But its activities were not entirely reactive. New places would sometimes be deliberately targeted, without any need for prior contacts. And although Lady Huntingdon does not seem to have made a systematic attempt to cover the whole country, she had aspirations to do so:

> What a sudden spread seems everywhere . . . I am now fitting out several able students to sound a general and universal alarm over England, in the fields and cities where the Gospel has not yet been sounded. I daily see our work is more and more universal, both from the leadings of God and also the lively and intrepid spirit of many . . . in this college . . . One young man has in one place a thousand constant hearers.

Lady Huntingdon to Mrs Haweis, 1 May 1774. Bridwell Library MS 82.

As the 1770s advanced, she was still planning new preaching initiatives. In 1778, for example, when she was in Devon recuperating after a fever, she had plans to take lodgings for a few days each in several places around Torbay, in order to see what openings there might be for an evangelistic campaign. In 1781 a small group of her clergy undertook a series of preaching tours through different parts of the country, in order (they said) to show that 'the New Reformation started more than forty years ago, does not yet stagnate'. Their intention, though not carried into effect, was to preach the gospel in every town and large village in the country, at least once a year. Glascott was one of these clergy. He started at Bristol in July, and went through Lincolnshire, Derbyshire and Yorkshire, before returning to Bristol in September. According to the detailed accounts he sent back to Lady Huntingdon, he preached in the open air, and in churches, in Dissenting meeting-houses, and in Connexion and other chapels. To his surprise, the latter even included an invitation to preach in a Wesleyan chapel. Sometimes he advertised his open-air preaching by placing a piece in the local paper, or by paying boys to announce it.

Glascott's preaching tour was a classic example of what is known as itinerant preaching: a tour covering large tracts of country, responding to opportunities as they offered, and combining open-air preaching with the use of borrowed premises where available. Similar examples occur from time to time over the following years. Nevertheless, Glascott's 1781 venture was already quite dated, so far as the Connexion was concerned. It was in fact inevitable that such informality would not remain the norm for very long. Signs of a more structured approach began to appear from an early stage in the Connexion's period of expansion. One example of this was the emergence of what became known as 'preaching rounds'. These were routes (more or less formalized) that preachers would take to ensure that preaching was followed up in places that had been visited before. References to rounds occur from the early 1770s, and some covered extensive areas – from 70 to 100 miles in some cases. A flavour of how a round could operate is given in this letter from one of the many lay people on whom the Connexion's local organization depended in different parts of the country. The two men referred to were both students, and the extract shows the demands that could be placed on students, once they were away from college:

I am in expectation of seeing another student everyday, as your Ladyship informs me of sending one this week, and may the Lord enable your Ladyship to send us one more, as four will not be [too many] for the many calls your Ladyship's students has from Weymouth to the western parts of Bridgewater round, which is about a hundred miles, and here are many more large and populous towns within few miles of this place who are destitute of the Gospel . . . Mr White and Holmes has preached without doors several times around this place . . . I would advise your Ladyship not to recall Mr White & Holmes from these rounds as yet, as they are so very extensive [&] they . . . don't know one half of the people.

Samuel Clark at South Petherton to Lady Huntingdon, 21 May 1774. F1/297, CF.

The Connexion's rounds developed in an informal way, in response to the needs of particular areas. They never represented a detailed parcelling up of the entire country, in the way that John Wesley attempted with Methodist circuits.

Open-air preaching was often the only way of starting off in an area, and it had the advantage both of flexibility and of being noticed. But the disadvantages were obvious, especially in winter. Nor was borrowing other people's buildings satisfactory in the longer term. So once a group of Connexion adherents had formed in a place, they would soon start thinking about acquiring their own premises. Some of the Connexion's ministers regretted this. Buildings tied people down, and were a sign that the Connexion was passing from its initial exuberance into a more mature, settled phase. The Revd Henry Peckwell, one of the new clergy-men who joined Lady Huntingdon in the 1770s, counselled her in 1774: 'Let us be more earnest in preaching than building this summer. It is impossible to supply the accumulating number of chapels.'

But the pressures to build could not be resisted, and with them came inevitable problems of finance. Many people assumed that countesses were automatically wealthy, and that Lady Huntingdon would provide the necessary funds. This was very seldom what happened, however, and occasionally there were recriminations when congregations realized that bills were down to them. Even in her initial phase of chapel building, in the 1760s, Lady Huntingdon had sometimes to look for financial assistance from others. From 1768 she was paying for Trevecca College as well. And yet her personal wealth was quite limited. She received only debts from her husband's estate, and there were long dis-putes over what, if anything, she was entitled to from her Ferrers relations. Where she could, she rented out the various houses she owned, and there were occasional gifts and legacies from friends – including (as we shall see in chapter 13) the American estates that she inherited from George Whitefield in 1770. But this was nothing like sufficient to fund the whole of the work that developed from the 1770s.

Sometimes Lady Huntingdon did give quite significant sums to new projects, however. In the early 1770s she contributed £100 each to several chapel-building funds. This should be set against the figure of around £250 which seems to have been the norm at that time for buying land and putting up a chapel in a medium-sized town. (Larger chapels, in major cities, could run into thousands of pounds.) The danger was that local congregations would over-stretch themselves on the (implied) security of her name, and that she would be left liable for any deficits. So she would seek clear guarantees as to a congregation's ability to raise its own share of the cost – rather as grant-giving bodies today may offer to match funds raised by local efforts. In the case of congregations in the Connexion, this might mean applying to other charitable bodies for help, or seeking help from richer chapels in one of the major cities. Or it might simply mean the members themselves saving up the money – something that was easier in the (rather rare) cases where the congregation included a few wealthier members.

Sometimes it was not newly formed but existing congregations that applied to join the Connexion. Such congregations might have been founded earlier on in the Revival. Or they might have been Dissenters without a current minister, or unhappy with the Dissenting ministers on offer. The attraction of the Connexion was both its orthodox Calvinist theology, and the apparent promise of regular ministerial supplies. Even so, however, admission to the Connexion was not automatic. Lady Huntingdon had to be satisfied that the congregation could pay its way, and had no excessive debts. The application to the Connexion in 1783 from a congregation in Rotherhithe is a good example of the process:

> The principal [trustee] came to me ... proposing to have [the chapel] conducted under your Ladyship's protection. Tis

a large handsome chapel, holds 12 or 1400; they suppose it would be crowded if our ministers were there & the Church service read. No large burden of debt upon it, but what might soon & easily be paid off ... I desired them ... to draw up a petition to your Ladyship requesting your patronage, & to take it entirely into the Connexion; & to be quite clear & explicit about all the circumstances of the lease, debt, disbursements, income etc.

The Revd Thomas Wills to Lady Huntingdon, 9 September 1783. F1/1901, CF.

In fact negotiations over the terms of Rotherhithe's entry to the Connexion took another month, with Wills insisting that Lady Huntingdon was to be exempt from any responsibility for their outstanding debt. (We shall look, in the next chapter, at the significance of that reference to the Connexion's use of the Church of England Prayer Book.)

The case of Rotherhithe is an illustration of how quickly the Countess of Huntingdon's Connexion became a distinct entity on the religious scene. It was not of course the only such group currently active. Interestingly, one of the issues that arose during the Rotherhithe negotiations was whether the congregation had previously tried to join the so-called 'Tabernacle Connexion', of George Whitefield's former followers. A striking feature of the Connexion was the extent to which it achieved near-national coverage. There were no major parts of England that were not touched by the Connexion at some time. The list of 64 principal chapels that was drawn up in 1790 included places in the Midlands, the south-west, the south-east, East Anglia, Lincolnshire, Yorkshire and Lancashire. The list did not include a number of congregations that had appeared regularly in preachers' letters a decade earlier, but which must subsequently have left the Connexion or folded altogether. This is a sign of how fluid Connexion membership could be.

Significant though the Connexion had become, its growth had been largely unplanned and haphazard. And that meant that its organization had to develop as it went along. We have seen already how preaching rounds grew up to try to maintain ministry to the various congregations that emerged as a result of itinerant preaching. But even with the aid of rounds, it was still a complex operation to ensure that all the various chapels and congregations were kept supplied with appropriate preachers. The task could not have been helped by the fact that Lady Huntingdon probably did not know, at any given time, exactly how many congregations the Connexion was serving. Nevertheless, allocating and distributing preachers was a task that Lady Huntingdon undertook personally in the great majority of cases, right up to the end of her life in 1791. Only in the last few years did she share some of the burden with a secretary, George Best, and a close friend, Lady Anne Erskine. But it was always *her* Connexion, and *her* preachers, and she never lost interest in the minutiae of what went on.

She had two main groups of men at her disposal: Anglican clergy and Trevecca students. A few clergymen worked for the Connexion full-time – for example, Glascott, whom we have met already, and Thomas Wills and William Taylor, who entered her full-time service in the later 1770s. The rest, including a group of Welsh clergy, generally had parishes of their own. This meant that Lady Huntingdon's plans had to fit with their availability, and often had to include finding other clergy to cover for them during their absences from home. As the Connexion grew over time, the arrangements for clergy became a little more formalized. In 1782 Lady Huntingdon described the system to one of her former students, who had by then been ordained in the Church of England:

In this Connexion there is a rotation of *Clergy*, throughout the large chapels and congregations. These serve some eight, some ten weeks in a congregation. Some of these have livings, and such are allowed two guineas a week, a lodging, and travelling charges (finding their own board), according to the time they serve in each congregation. Should you like to make trial of one of these, by way of trial only, at any time, you can have your church supplied. Let me know, and I will appoint you.

Lady Huntingdon to James Glazebrook, 13 September 1782. Quoted in *Life & Times of the Countess of Huntingdon*, ii, 90.

Different considerations applied so far as her current students were concerned. And here too there were significant constraints on her freedom of action. She had limited control, for example, over the number of students at any one time who were of a sufficient standard to be sent out preaching. She had to work out the logistics (including the cost) of getting them from the college in Wales to the most distant parts of England. She had to match what she knew of their skills to the needs of the congregations to whom they were sent: for example, if they were native Welsh speakers, how fluent they were in English. And she had to take into account practical considerations, like whether to hire or buy horses, and how to keep her young men away from places where they might be press-ganged into the Navy.

There are many examples of the detailed instructions that Lady Huntingdon sent to her students, as well as the interest she took in their well-being. The following extracts from letters she sent to one student, Robert McAll, illustrate both of these aspects, as well as her expectation of absolute obedience. (The last of the three letters was written in the final year of her life.)

... the state of your health obliges my most express direction to set out for London upon receiving these instructions ... A horse is wanted for the Devonshire Round, so instead of your selling it, travel with it to Putcham in the neighbourhood of Bridgewater and leave it for Mr Theophilus Jones at Mr Spurier's in Putcham, and then come by coach to London.

Mr Denham evidently being called from Brighton, I have appointed you to succeed on Sunday the tenth *without fail*, then Mr Jones to Reading and Mr Williams to Wallingford. This prevents the expense of more distant removes, and on your receiving this, desire that you set out for London, as you may serve on your way.

Your letter gave me much uneasiness from the situation . . . of your health. My object for my ministers is as much ease and comfort for their bodies as is consistent with the daily cross of the Son of God . . . On your receiving this, set out for Swansea: I know the sea air, in your case, will be great relief, & what minister is arrived there send off to Gloucester.

Lady Huntingdon to Robert McAll, 13 September 1788, 5 May 1789, & 2 October 1790. E4/17(2–4), CF.

It is interesting, though perhaps not surprising, that Lady Huntingdon sometimes lost track of who was serving at a particular place – as the last of these extracts shows. Just occasionally she seems to have forgotten about people altogether, leaving them with the same congregation for a year or more – until the preacher, or his hearers, wrote to ask for a change. Other sorts of mistake occurred, the most common being when a congregation was left without a preacher at all – which could sometimes be for weeks on end.

Lady Huntingdon clearly regarded the posting of preachers as one of her key functions, and only rarely did she share it with anyone else. She was certainly right in seeing this as a vital means of keeping control of her Connexion, since so much depended on the skills, personalities and theology of individual preachers. How far this was a selfish desire to hang onto her authority, and how far an honest belief that God was best served with her in charge, is impossible to say. There were a few occasions on which Anglican clergy were allowed to decide on the distribution of available preachers within the locality in which they themselves were working. And prominent local laymen might sometimes have a say over how the small congregations in a round were to be served. But that was about it.

As the years went by, there appeared an unintended but significant challenge to Lady Huntingdon's control of the Connexion. This was when congregations and preachers grew tired of itinerancy, and pushed for a more settled form of ministry. It cannot generally have been very satisfactory for congregations to have their ministers changed after very short spaces of time. It meant they were continually having to get used to a new face, and a new style of preaching, and that they were continually worried about being left with a vacancy. And it was difficult to persuade wealthier supporters to make a longer-term financial commitment to chapel funds, when no-one knew who the preachers would be, even a few months ahead. Only when a congregation wanted to get rid of an unsuitable preacher would there have seemed much attraction in the system of rotation. Even then, congregations might have argued that if they had chosen their minister in the first place, rather than relying on whomever Lady Huntingdon happened to send, then questions of unsuitability would have been less likely to arise.

For preachers, too, there were arguments for being settled with a specific congregation, or group of congregations. At the start of their careers, especially if they were still single, itinerancy might be an attractive option. It offered challenge and excitement, and it involved going out to preach the gospel in a very literal way. It also offered the chance to leave mistakes behind, and start afresh using the lessons learned. But after a while, it could begin to pall. For the students, and for ministers serving full-time in the Connexion, it was a hard, isolated and homeless existence, with little chance to put down roots. Cradock Glascott summed it up:

I am now in the tenth year of my itinerancy, & am without house or home. I begin to wish some place of residence of my own during the winter, & would hope to continue rambling as before [in] the summer months. I have nothing yet in view, but hope Providence will soon point out some place for me. I have lately thought more favourably of matrimony ... although I am not yet fixed in my choice of a yoke-fellow ... Your Ladyship will I trust excuse the freedom I have taken to write on this subject ... I should be sorry to take any step that may lessen me in your Ladyship's esteem.

Glascott to Lady Huntingdon, 1 June 1776. F1/1729, CF.

The solution for Glascott, a few years later, was acceptance of a parish in Devon, combined (when Lady Huntingdon had eventually forgiven him) with occasional service in the Connexion. For the students – especially after the Connexion had started its own form of ordination in 1783 (see chapter 15) – it was often invitations from individual congregations that offered an escape from continual travelling. Such invitations might come from one of the Connexion's own congregations. Or they might be from an established congregation outside the Connexion, who liked what they had heard about a particular minister. Requests to settle with a congregation were not initially welcomed by Lady Huntingdon, because they undermined her means of exercising her authority. They threatened to turn her centrally regulated Connexion into a loose amalgamation of independent churches. Once a man settled with a congregation, he ceased to be a fully flexible resource, available to be sent wherever she wished. The most she could hope for was that he would provide occasional help elsewhere in the Connexion.

Nevertheless, the pressure to settle was too great to be resisted. By the early 1780s it was becoming the natural progression for more experienced ministers, after they had served their 'probation' as full-time itinerants. Itinerancy did not disappear;

interestingly, its benefits began to be recognized within Dissent around this time. But in the Connexion it became merely an adjunct to the more general pattern of ministers serving specific congregations.

We have looked in this chapter at the ways in which Lady Huntingdon's congregations started off and became established, and at how she sought to manage them from the centre. In the next chapter we shall look at some of the features of life within the congregations themselves.

11

What It Was Like to Belong to a Countess of Huntingdon Congregation

❦

Within most of the congregations linked to Lady Huntingdon there were two sub-groups that made an important contribution to the organization's corporate life. The first of these consisted of the congregation's local organizers. Although Lady Huntingdon took charge of the posting of preachers, there were still many jobs for local congregations to do, like finding accommodation for preachers and handling their expenses – not to mention the vital task of maintaining contact with the Countess herself. Then there were the congregation's own affairs to manage, especially if they had their own premises: there were funds to be raised, repairs to be carried out, debts to be serviced, and so on. Sometimes the main burden of such work would fall on an individual member of the congregation. In some cases this might be the same person who had invited the preachers initially.

More often a committee would emerge, and this could be more than just an administrative device. In one case, a committee was described as 'the people's voice for regulating the Chapel' – which implied that it was seen, in a sense, as the representative of the congregation, in its dealings both with Lady Huntingdon and with individual ministers. This did not mean that committees were directly elected, or that one could be appointed without Lady Huntingdon's agreement. But it did mean that a congregation had a means of arguing its case with her. In at least one case a committee resigned in protest at decisions Lady Huntingdon had taken. Ministers might also act in ways of which a committee disapproved. Their conduct of the services might not fit with the traditions of the chapel, they might claim excessive expenses, or their preaching might not be up to scratch. Committees provided a means of voicing and responding to such concerns. For that reason, some of the Connexion's ministers were suspicious of the power of committees. They feared they might become like deacons in some Dissenting churches, and tyrannize their preachers. An important issue, in the battles that arose towards the end of Lady Huntingdon's life over the future organization of her Connexion, was how to achieve a proper balance between the interests of congregations and preachers.

An example of the sort of disagreements that could arise between ministers and congregations, and of the role that committees might play in preventing them, is shown in the following extract. The author had recently arrived to serve the Chichester chapel.

Yesterday in the afternoon I was sent for, and waited upon Mr Dearling, who has withdrawn from the chapel for some time ... Some of his reasons [for withdrawing] were these, that the rules of the chapel were so often broke through, & that the managers had no power to act so as to keep them inviolable. But the principal reason was that the minister had invited and administered the ordinance [i.e., Holy Communion] to as many as had arrived to partake – and that without acquainting the Church of [it], which was contrary to their rules ... The minister said that was ... the way he would proceed ... [Dearling's] sentiment is that none should communicate but the members & those that have proposed themselves as such ... His desire is that the committee should have power to keep the rules of a church inviolable.

David Pritchard to Lady Huntingdon, 14 November 1783. F1/567, CF.

The reference in that extract to the 'Church' and to 'members' brings us to the other important group within many congregations. Almost certainly a distinction was being made between the general congregation who turned up for Sunday services, and an inner core of church members who would meet together at other times to develop their spiritual life. We saw earlier how so-called 'religious societies' appeared in the Church of England in the late seventeenth century, and contributed to the spiritual climate out of which the Evangelical Revival developed. The idea of holding informal meetings to stimulate the faith of participants is of course a pretty obvious one, and the practice was quickly taken up within the Revival. In the case of evangelical parishes in the Church of England, such meetings were likely to be clergy-led and were often held in the parsonage. They formed a distinct part of the teaching programme of the parish. John Newton at Olney, for example, held a weekday lecture, a children's class, and twice-weekly prayer meetings. He commented about this inner core of his congregation, 'I preach to many, but those whose hearts the Lord touches are the people of my peculiar charge.'

Outside the Church of England, participation in such extra-curricular activity tended to be more formalized. In Wesleyan Methodism, for example, the arrangements could be very formal indeed, with society meetings divided into smaller bands and classes, so that members could talk freely to each other about their spiritual progress – or lack of it. References to societies appear from an early stage in the development of the Countess's Connexion, in one case being described, interestingly, as 'a society or serious meeting'. Societies were often regarded as a means of strengthening a congregation, by building up the faith of its most committed members. Sometimes they appeared quite soon after a congregation had been formed; in other cases years might elapse before a society was introduced. Only society members could attend society meetings, and admission to membership was taken to imply that a certain degree of religious maturity had been reached. Practice varied as to whether any formal test was imposed on would-be members; sometimes applicants were put through a prior examination as to their experience of God.

We hear most about societies in the case of the larger chapels, where the numbers involved meant that a substantial amount of activity was possible. In some cases there were even separate men's and women's society meetings each week, in addition to a meeting of the whole society and some mid-week public services. In smaller country districts, the pattern of meetings was likely to be much less, with the members more reliant on their own resources, rather than on input from a minister or student. But the society could still play a significant role in the members' non-working lives – and also (as in the case at Chichester) serve to defend the ethos and traditions of the chapel.

The following extract gives an idea of the controls and expectations that societies placed on their members, especially at chapels served by one of Lady Huntingdon's senior clergymen:

I had a general meeting of the [Brighton] society last Wednesday . . . in particular I recommended that if any had a quarrel against any that they should not suffer it to canker in their breast, but that they should go to the party concerned . . . If that had not the desired effect, let him take two or three of the most prudent of the society . . . & repeat the offence before them. If this does not avail, let him carry his complaint to the resident minister, who in conjunction with a properly selected number . . . may finally decide who is in the right & who in the wrong. If the offending party will not then submit, let him be dismissed from the society . . . I intend moreover to hold a love-feast here on Monday senight week . . . that . . . their hearts may imperceptibly warm towards each other.

. . . all the differences are in a fair way to be entirely healed & . . . our love-feast was remarkably blessed to that end . . . I am grieved that I was obliged to take Humphrey the tailor's ticket from him for he came to the love-feast very drunk. I cannot help wishing that there were five or six of the most solid of the society appointed to inspect the walk and conversation of the rest & make weekly their report to the resident minister . . . If those of a superior condition in life would not choose to submit their conduct to one perhaps of an inferior degree . . . [they] might be visited by the minister who would not have leisure to overlook the whole society . . . himself.

The Revd Walter Shirley to Lady Huntingdon, 7 & 23 July 1770. F1/1503 & 1561, CF.

'Love-feasts', referred to in that passage, were an idea revived by the Moravians from the fellowship meals practised in the Early Church. Wesleyans and Whitefieldites both made frequent use of love-feasts, but in the Connexion they are only found occasionally, and at the major chapels. Even then, they appear to be for a specific purpose, like praying for the Connexion or (as here) for settling differences among the society's members.

Love-feasts were not the same as Holy Communion, which was highly prized right across the Connexion. Unlike John Wesley – who for a long time held to the principle that his followers should take Communion in their parish churches, rather than on their own premises – Lady Huntingdon had no scruple about Communion services being held in her chapels. The main constraint, until the Connexion introduced its own ordination in 1783 (see chapter 15, below) was the availability of ordained men to lead Communion services. There was never any question of the students, or other lay people, administering Communion. At the larger chapels that were regularly supplied by clergymen, Communion services might be very frequent – even weekly, as happened at Bath in the 1770s. (This, incidentally, put the Connexion on a par with some of the best practice in the Church of England: in many parts of the country, parish churches

thought they were doing well to have a monthly Communion.)
The best that most of the Connexion's congregations could hope
for was a Communion every couple of months, and even that
might not always be sustainable. But regular opportunities to
take Communion were something the Connexion's members
valued very highly. So after 1783 Lady Huntingdon often received
requests for individual students to be ordained, so that the
congregation concerned could receive the sacraments.

As implied by the row at Chichester, mentioned above, it was
generally thought right to restrict admission to Communion to
the inner core of society members – and no exception to this
seems to have been considered for those who were communicants at other churches. Communion might take place in private,
or in front of the whole congregation. What was important was
that communicants should be in a fit state to receive the sacraments, and there is occasional evidence of ministers taking active
steps to ensure that people were properly prepared:

> ... our little Church is in a flourishing condition, the mem-
> bership thereof being forty in number ... Last Lord's Day
> was the first time of celebrating the Lord's supper. The reason
> why it was postponed so long was the deficiency of most of
> the members in the clear, distinct knowledge of the mysteries
> of Christ ... their not having a completeness of Evangelical
> knowledge to discern the Lord's body. I have taken as much
> care and pains in examination, and instructing of all that have
> been admitted as I could.

Thomas Molland to Lady Huntingdon, 28 August 1777. F1/402, CF.

It was frequently the practice for the Connexion to use the
Church of England Prayer Book for its public services. Examples
of this are found in many parts of the country, and in some of the
less significant chapels as well as the major ones. Sometimes this
would simply have been due to habit or to affection for the Church

prayers. But in other cases the Prayer Book was used because it gave the Connexion an aura of respectability and implied a basic loyalty to the doctrines of the Established Church. In a sense this meant that the Connexion offered the best of all worlds to people who were loyal to the Church of England, but who wanted the evangelical teaching that they could not find in their parish church: Church of England clergy, using Church of England liturgy, but preaching the doctrines of the Revival.

Not all the Connexion's adherents agreed about the attractiveness of the Prayer Book, however. Some congregations preferred freer forms of prayer, and found the Prayer Book too staid and formalized for their liking. Some even thought it smacked of popery. Just occasionally Lady Huntingdon allowed individual ministers to decide, in the light of local circumstances, whether to have the Prayer Book or not. Despite these variations in practice, however, use of the Prayer Book remained one of the distinctive features of the Connexion. Even at the start of the nineteenth century, a decade after Lady Huntingdon's death, it was still in use at all the Connexion's principal chapels.

As well as praying like clergymen, the Connexion's ministers (including the students) often dressed like them as well. That is, they wore gowns and preaching bands. When a student received his gown, it was a sign of his membership of the college and the Connexion; conversely, being required to give up one's gown was a powerful symbol of Lady Huntingdon's displeasure. Wearing a gown brought clear practical benefits, because it implied status and authority. This could be an important factor when facing opposition, as one student, Anthony Crole, discovered in 1774:

Last Sunday morning I preached among them at Corfe Castle, there were . . . upward of two thousand people, in a field belonging to the Quakers . . . The curate of Corfe has preached one sermon against us at the three different churches on the Island, wherein he bitterly inveighs against the enthusiasts &

illegal preachers of this day. I found my gown & bands was looked upon by the poor people as a sufficient refutation of the curate's sermon.

Crole to Lady Huntingdon, 13 July 1774. F1/311, CF.

If the Connexion looked Anglican in its liturgy and in the way its ministers dressed, it was a typical part of the Evangelical Revival when it came to singing hymns. Hymns were important not only because they made services more varied and attractive. Just as significantly they reinforced the doctrines and religious attitudes that were taught in sermons. Having collections of theologically correct hymns was therefore important. Of course there were many hymns that could be sung quite happily by all sections of the Revival, as well as by Christians outside it. Through John Wesley's translations, a number of Moravian hymns entered the Revival and have become a part of the English worshipping heritage. The same applies, to an even greater extent, to some of Charles Wesley's hymns. But hymns could touch on theologically sensitive issues. Lady Huntingdon would not want her congregations singing hymns praising Christian Perfection, as taught by the Wesleys, any more than the latter would want hymns that proclaimed Calvinist beliefs.

Lady Huntingdon herself wrote some hymns, though it is often difficult to be confident about the authorship of hymns ascribed to her. One hymn that was certainly by her is called 'Blow ye the trumpet'. It contains the following lines which, while firmly asserting that salvation is through Christ alone, contain few of the overtly Calvinist overtones that might have alienated Wesley's followers:

Exalt the Lamb of God,
The all-atoning Lamb;
Redemption by his blood
Thro' all the world proclaim:

The year of Jubilee is come;
Return, ye ransom'd sinners, home.

Ye who have sold for nought
Your heritage above,
Shall have it back, unbought,
The gift of Jesus' love:
The year, etc.

'Supplement to Dr Watts's *Psalms & Hymns*, primarily designed for the use of the congregation assembling in the chapel adjoining the Hoxton Academy, London' (first compiled in 1807).

The Hoxton Academy, from whose book that hymn is quoted, was an evangelical Dissenting college – one of a number that came into existence in the late eighteenth century, inspired by the example of Trevecca. The fact that Lady Huntingdon's hymn turned up in their book is a sign of how quickly hymns move across denominational boundaries.

As early as 1768 the Connexion had its own hymn-book on sale. The book was primarily designed for use in the Connexion's own chapels, although clergy associated with the Connexion occasionally used it in their parish churches. Meeting the needs of the whole Connexion meant that lots of copies were needed: even in 1769, when the Connexion's era of expansion was only just beginning, at least 2,000 copies were reprinted. Lady Huntingdon seems to have met the start-up costs, on the assumption that the book would eventually become self-financing through sales. Producing and distributing the book was a significant operation. Requests from congregations for copies, debates about what to charge, and fears of being under-cut by pirated editions, all appear in Lady Huntingdon's correspondence from time to time.

Over the years the book passed through a number of editions. It was perhaps inevitable (given that few subjects raise stronger emotions among Christians than the choice of hymns) that there should be arguments about what should or should not be included. In 1773, for example, Walter Shirley, who was working on a new edition, wanted to cut out hymns that he thought involved 'vile doggerel and hum-drum tunes'. Whichever these were, Lady Huntingdon wanted to keep them – and Lady Huntingdon won the argument. And notwithstanding all the traumas, the hymn-book eventually turned in a profit that went to support other aspects of the Connexion's work.

One other aspect of the life of congregations needs to be mentioned: their work (or lack of it) with children. Interest in the spiritual care of children was something to which the Revival gave particular attention, although such concern was not confined to them. In the Church of England at large, for example, it was not uncommon for parishes to instruct children in the meaning of the Catechism, before they were presented for Confirmation. Indeed, the Prayer Book required them to do so. (The Catechism is a set of questions about the principal Christian doctrines and duties, which has been part of the Anglican Prayer Book since 1549.) Wesley's Holy Club developed this idea, combining religious and secular teaching through a school that instructed children in reading and the Catechism. John Newton tried using a children's group as a tool in his efforts to evangelize his parish at Olney, hoping that the children's enthusiasm (encouraged by little gifts) would stimulate interest on the part of the parents. Lady Huntingdon tried a rather similar device at Brighton in the mid 1760s, using a group of about 30 children to try to reach some of the most destitute children in the town. Unfortunately, we do not know how successful Lady Huntingdon's 'gang' proved to be.

Despite this innovative approach, Lady Huntingdon's interest in children's work seems to have waned, once she got more actively involved in adult ministry. There is a surprising dearth of references to children's work during the Connexion's years of expansion. This could be because ministers felt that such activity was too obvious to mention, but their letters covered so many detailed aspects of congregational life that this seems unlikely. In the 1780s the position changed a bit, possibly inspired by the much-publicized example of the Sunday School founded by Raymond Raikes in Gloucester in 1781. This offered general education, as well as religious instruction. In 1784 leading members of the Bath congregation established a school attached to the chapel. By 1788 the committee calculated that this had educated some 70 poor children. In the same year the large London chapel Spa Fields (see chapter 15, below) reported that they had had 80 through their school, which had started only two years earlier. As at Bath, the initiative for this came from lay people at the chapel, rather than from Lady Huntingdon, who clearly had reservations about anything that she thought might deflect resources from other areas of her work. In 1788 she sparked a serious row with the Bath chapel committee, by insisting that the school and the chapel be run as separate institutions.

There were a few other instances of educational initiatives in the Connexion. But overall it has to be said that the Connexion's record in this area was decidedly patchy.

We looked in the previous chapter at how new chapels were funded, and saw that Lady Huntingdon sometimes made contributions herself. It was a rather similar picture so far as chapels' on-going costs were concerned. The general idea was that chapels should be self-supporting, but there is evidence, through the 1770s and 1780s, of Lady Huntingdon giving occasional financial help to individual chapels. At other times she donated ecclesiastical items, like the silver necessary for Communion services. There seems to have been no systematic approach to Lady Huntingdon's giving: she just reacted spontaneously when a need was brought to her attention. Sometimes others made commitments on her behalf. The result was that expectations could be raised that she was unable to meet. The recriminations could then be bitter, as shown in this letter to her secretary from an angry member of the Birmingham chapel committee:

> I must beg you will request her Ladyship to make choice of some person to supply my place in the committee, as I cannot prevail upon myself to continue any longer in a situation that seems a trap calculated to involve myself and family in future difficulties ... We have had the most solemn promises of assistance held out to us, even under her Ladyship's own hand ... but when this promised assistance is applied for, the utmost we get is a letter none of us can well understand. I therefore will be duped no longer ... Not the one of us knew for months after we engaged in this business that the whole purchase money was to be left as a burden on us, but expected, as her Ladyship reserved the presentation to the pulpit in her own hands, that she had really bought it. However, all I wish for now is an indemnification for what I stand engaged; this is no more than was at first promised by Mr Wills.

S. Seager to George Best, 12 November 1788. F1/782, CF.

Congregations were not the only aspect of the Connexion that cost money. Students and ministers had to be paid for as well. So far as the students out preaching were concerned, Lady Huntingdon seems initially to have borne the whole financial responsibility. She regularly received invoices from the students themselves, or from congregations, in respect of the money they had spent. A major item was travel and accommodation, since the accounts suggest that it could cost around £1 a week to keep a student on the road. Clothes were another significant amount: on one occasion Lady Huntingdon received a bill for over £6 for a suit and a greatcoat that an individual student had decided he needed. In order to keep a check on students' extravagance, the processing of their expenses was sometimes delegated to ministers or local congregations – though still with Lady Huntingdon footing the bill.

As time went on, responsibility for supporting the students rightly devolved onto congregations, although the change-over seems to have taken place gradually, and not in any clear or coordinated way. As early as 1773, for example, Lady Huntingdon was told of a congregation that thought students' expenses should be met locally – yet the cost of supporting student preachers seems generally to have stayed with her for some time after that date. It was a rather similar story with the clergy who preached for the Connexion. By the late 1770s it was clearly up to some congregations to pay for their clergy. This included deciding whether or not to fund curates to provide home cover for the beneficed clergy who gave them occasional help. Yet for some years after that, Lady Huntingdon was still supporting ministry at other chapels, including contributing to the cost of curates. This confused picture is a sign of the autocratic way in which Lady Huntingdon ran the Connexion. Because she had no central conference or committee to assist her, changes tended to be made in a piecemeal fashion. Unlike the Wesleyans, who published reports of the conclusions at their annual conferences, there were no Connexion minutes to record decisions – because there was no formal process to reach decisions in the first place.

How much might be paid to support a full-time minister depended on a congregation's circumstances. Lady Huntingdon's rule of thumb was £100 a year, plus a house – a figure in line with what a poor (though not the poorest) beneficed Anglican clergyman might expect. Many small-town Connexion congregations, however, managed less than half that figure. As well as paying for their minister, there were other recurring costs that congregations had to meet, of which a major one would be either rent, or interest charges on loans taken out to purchase or extend their premises.

If they were to meet their outgoings, congregations had to formalize their fund-raising, especially if they had few afflu-ent members to bear the main burden. An obvious way would have been to have regular collections at services, but there was a strange reluctance (especially on Lady Huntingdon's part) to agree to this too often. A quarterly collection came to be regarded as about the norm. The more frequently used device was the sale of season tickets for reserved seats in the chapel. Tickets promised a significant source of income, and the prospect of regular attendance. But they obviously limited the number of free seats that were available, and some people found this objectionable. Tickets meant that the poor had the worst seats, and they also damaged a chapel's outreach by discouraging newcomers. In some cases there might even be different ticket prices, depending on the quality of the seats on offer:

From the first erecting [of the Connexion chapel in Bristol] we have been not only hearers of God's word and partakers of his blessed ordinance ... but we had also the privilege to meet in your Ladyship's chapel for prayer and at the private meeting also ... [Our purpose in writing] is to represent to your Ladyship the mercenary proceedings now going forward in your Ladyship's chapel, which is now become more like a play-house than the house of God – for first there are tickets for the throne, then the pit or red seats next the pen, a few benches for God's poor saints, then the gallery – four or five being employed to sell tickets on the Sabbath ... There is no place free now in the chapel but a dark dismal hole under the gallery, more like a corner of Newgate than any part of God's house. This we attribute all to [the minister currently serving Bristol] ... being an entire stranger to the way of God sending out the Methodist[s] at first ... Your Ladyship well knoweth that that much honoured servant of God Mr Whitefield always made it his study to make room for the poor ... And not only the poor, but many other who sometimes drop in ... out of curiosity.

Members of the Bristol chapel society to Lady Huntingdon, 4 February 1778. F1/1816, CF.

Tickets would normally be issued for three months at a time, and the four occasions in the year when they came up for renewal naturally became key points in the annual calendar. It was vital to maximize attendance on renewal days, so chapels would want a good preacher that day, as well as trying to avoid clashing with competing attractions elsewhere in the locality. There could be heated complaints to Lady Huntingdon if her directions for the rotation of ministers meant that a chapel was unsupplied at the time the tickets were due for renewal.

Another source of complaint would be if Lady Huntingdon ordered a collection for the so-called 'Travelling Fund' at the same time as the new quarterly tickets went on sale. The Travelling Fund was established in the early 1780s, principally to pay for work in new areas and in poorer parts of the country. It was run initially from Spa Fields chapel in London and it was separate from Lady Huntingdon's own finances – although on at least one occasion she received a 'present' from the Fund in respect of her ministers' expenses. Collections were its main source of income, however, and it was Lady Huntingdon who decided when and where Travelling Fund collections were to be held. The existence of the Fund was intended to ensure that the major chapels bore some of the central costs of the Connexion, although in practice the lion's share was carried by Spa Fields. What the Travelling Fund did not address was congregations' own building and running expenses, so the big chapels still regularly received appeals for help from their struggling brethren – again, with Spa Fields receiving the majority of requests.

It is very difficult to generalize about life in the Connexion, despite Lady Huntingdon's efforts to control so much of what went on. This is because its different congregations varied enormously in their situation, size and expectations. There were chapels in major centres of population that were served by some of the best evangelical preachers of the day – and there were tiny rural congregations who were lucky even to get a share in the ministry of an inexperienced student. There was Spa Fields chapel at the centre, turning over hundreds of pounds each year – and there were provincial congregations who struggled to raise a fraction of that amount. They all (for most of the time) acknowledged Lady Huntingdon's authority, but here again there were differences. Some congregations knew her personally and well. But for the majority she was an unseen power – probably regarded much as the Queen-Empress would be, a century later, in the remoter corners of the Raj.

We shall look, in a later chapter, at the (unsuccessful) attempts that were to be made, towards the end of Lady Huntingdon's life, to create a coherent structure for the longer-term organization of these very different elements.

12

Rows with Wesley

❧

In the last two chapters we have looked at the way the Connexion
operated and expanded in the two decades following the
founding of Trevecca College in 1768. We now need to resume
the chronological account of Lady Huntingdon's career by examining two significant developments that both started in 1770: the
doctrinal quarrel that split the Revival, following the Conference
Minutes which Wesley published that year, and the start of the
Connexion's work in America. We shall look at the first of these
in this chapter.

We saw at the start of this book that there was an unresolved
– and irresolvable – theological dilemma at the heart of the
Evangelical Revival. It is worth recalling that issue again, since
we cannot properly appreciate the feelings that arose on the two
sides, if we focus simply on predestination. It was certainly true
that Lady Huntingdon believed in predestination, while John
Wesley did not. But we need to realize why predestination came
up at all. To do so we need to go back to the belief, shared by all
evangelicals, that all human beings since Adam were so inher-
ently sinful that they could only be saved by an undeserved act of
love on God's part. The problem was in deciding the basis upon
which some were saved, and others were not. Did human beings
have any part to play in the process, or not? If they *did*, then it
could be said that they had in some sense 'earned' or 'bought'
their salvation. That seemed to some evangelicals to make human
effort more significant than Christ's achievement on the Cross.

Worse still, it implied that man had the final say over whether he was saved or not (in theological terms, that man was 'sovereign', rather than God).

This was where predestination came in, because it offered a different explanation of how salvation worked. Those who believed in predestination (it is convenient to call them 'Calvinists', although the doctrine can be traced back to the New Testament) said that it was not human beings who somehow qualified them-selves for salvation. It was God, in his love, who picked out some individuals to receive the gift of salvation that *nobody* deserved. This is fine, of course, if you focus on those on the receiving end of salvation – and it was the generous and comforting aspects of the doctrine that moderate Calvinists sought to emphasize. But the opponents of predestination could not ignore the broader picture, or the unfairness it seemed to imply. If some people were chosen, that meant that the rest were not. It made God into a fickle tyrant, handing out Heaven to some, and Hell to others, without discrimination. God's love was turned into a lottery. Those who opposed Calvinism were generally termed 'Arminians', after the sixteenth-century Dutch theologian Jacobus Arminius, who had taught that belief in human free-will was not incompatible with God's sovereignty.

This is as fundamental a theological question as you could find, and yet there is no *logical* way out of it. It is one of those unanswerable conundrums with which the Church has lived for two millennia. Such debates are always likely to be a significant issue in any movement like the Evangelical Revival which sets particular store on personal salvation. The fact that the Revival got through three decades without a cataclysmic split over these issues is a sign that the leaders recognized that it was better to live with unresolved differences than to push them to a conclu-sion that was unlikely to be achievable. After an early skirmish in the 1740s they tried, by and large, to avoid public controversy. As we have seen, there were periodic attempts to develop common strategies and to promote harmony. Where coolness can be observed between those of differing theological views, it was as much to do with personalities as with doctrines. So, in the later 1760s, there were many instances of warm personal regard between John Wesley and some of the leading Calvinist evangelicals, especially George Whitefield. When Whitefield was in America in 1770, on what proved his final visit, Wesley gave him authority in respect of the Wesleyan preachers in that country:

> I must beg of you to [encourage] our preachers as you judge best, who are as yet comparatively young and inexperienced, by giving them such advices as you think proper, and, above all, by exhorting them, not only to love one another, but, if it be possible, as much as lies in them to live peaceably with all men.

Wesley to Whitefield, 21 February 1770. *Letters*, v, 184.

This was a significant acknowledgement on Wesley's part of the common objectives that they both shared. Whitefield's followers returned the compliment, after Whitefield's death a few months later, by inviting Wesley to preach a funeral sermon on his old friend. He called Whitefield 'that blessed man' (in the strict sense of that expression, and not as a pejorative!).

Lady Huntingdon also had close friendships across the doctrinal divide. An obvious example of this was Charles Wesley. It is also striking that she chose an Arminian, John Fletcher, to be the first president of her college. In early 1770 she added another Arminian to the teaching staff, a young man called Joseph Benson, who had previously taught classics at Wesley's school, Kingswood. But with John Wesley himself matters were different. In their later lives neither of them could recapture the warmth that had characterized their early relationship. It was not simply that their organizations were potential rivals: the same could be said of Wesley and Whitefield. It just seems that Lady Huntingdon and

John Wesley could not really trust each other. Wesley was not one of the many friends she consulted about her plans for Trevecca, even though it was arguably the most significant development in her life to date. She probably had no illusions as to the doubts he had about the college, even though he agreed to preach there on the first anniversary of its opening.

Given all the sensitivities, why did Wesley take a step in 1770 that was almost guaranteed to provoke a hostile reaction from Calvinists like Lady Huntingdon? In part the answer may be that Wesley could sometimes be remarkably (or deliberately) naïve when it came to anticipating how people would react to him. It was also the case that the differences between Calvinists and Arminians had been brought into prominence by the St Edmund Hall affair. The students' supposed Calvinist beliefs were an issue in the case against them – so Wesley could comfort himself that the expulsions had effectively confirmed that the University's formal doctrinal position was akin to his own. But subsequent publications by Sir Richard Hill and the Revd Augustus Toplady were a stark reminder that there were articulate Anglicans around, ready to propound full-blooded Calvinist beliefs. Toplady's 1769 publication, for example, bore the defiant title: *The Doctrine of Absolute Predestination Stated and Asserted.* All this was anathema to Wesley, and not just because it propounded a harsh view of God's justice. Almost worse was the fact that such beliefs did not allow account to be taken of personal behaviour. It implied that God was not interested in whether people performed good works or not, nor whether they were growing in personal holiness. And enabling the believer to pursue holiness was (for Wesley) one of the chief reasons for the foundation of Methodism in the first place.

At his Annual Conference in August 1770, Wesley tackled head-on the relationship between good works and salvation. A few extracts from the published minutes give a flavour of his approach:

We have received it as a maxim that 'a man is to do nothing in order to justification.' Nothing can be more false. Whoever desires to find favour with God should 'cease from evil and learn to do well.' Whoever repents should do 'works meet for repentance.' And if this is not *in order* to find favour, what does he do them for? . . .

Is this not salvation by works?

Not by the *merit* of works, but by works as a *condition*.

What have we, then, been disputing about for these thirty years?

I am afraid about words . . .

We are every hour and every moment pleasing or displeasing to God 'according to our works' – according to the whole of our inward tempers, and our outward behaviour.

From the Minutes of the 27th Methodist Conference, 7–10 August 1770.

There is no reason to suppose that the published Minutes were aimed personally at Lady Huntingdon. But the Minutes reached her very quickly, and she reacted strongly against them (possibly burning her copy in disgust). They fuelled her general distrust of Wesley and his motives. She informed him that he would not be welcome at the 1770 college anniversary, and seems to have regarded his planned attendance there as a sinister bid to gain influence over the students. A tactful approach on Wesley's part might have enabled him to persuade Lady Huntingdon that he was not the heretic she supposed him – and thus have contained, at an early stage, what became a rift affecting the whole Revival. But Wesley chose this, of all moments, to send Lady Huntingdon a letter of advice that he claimed to have been contemplating for a long time. The text of this letter has not survived, but it evidently laid into everything from her personal pride, to the doggerel of some of the hymns in the Connexion's hymn-book. Wesley claimed to have been 'speaking the truth in love'. It is usually worrying when Christians say this, and even some of Wesley's friends thought the letter ill-judged. At around the same time he sent a letter to Joseph Benson which seems to demonstrate his ability for both self-delusion and self-satisfaction, where Lady Huntingdon was concerned. Benson was at this stage still hanging on as master at Trevecca College:

> I am glad you had the courage to speak your mind [to Lady Huntingdon.] At all hazards do so still, only with all possible tenderness and respect. She is much devoted to God and has a thousand valuable and amiable qualities. There is no great fear that I should be prejudiced against one whom I have intimately known for these thirty years. And I know what is in man; therefore I make large allowance for human weaknesses. But what you say is exactly the state of the case. They are 'jealous of their authority.' Truly there is no cause ... I fear and shun, not desire, authority of any kind. Only when God lays that burthen upon me, I bear it for His and the people's sake.

Wesley to Benson, 5 October 1770. *Letters*, v, 202–3.

The news of Whitefield's death, which reached England in November, led to a shared sense of loss right across the Revival. Nevertheless, divisions were gradually opening up, the immediate focus being Trevecca College. Joseph Benson survived there for a while longer, despite making no secret of his links with Wesley and his sympathy with Wesley's theology. But in December Lady Huntingdon challenged him on the key issues of human free-will, and whether salvation was offered to all. Benson could not satisfy her on these points, and was dismissed early in 1771. Fletcher continued as president of Trevecca till March. But when the whole student body was required to write a response to the Minutes – with the threat that Lady Huntingdon would expel anyone 'who did not *absolutely* disavow and renounce' them – he could not honourably stay silent. His own detailed justification of the Minutes was also his letter of resignation.

At this stage reaction to the Minutes was largely confined to Lady Huntingdon's circle, and it was some time before others followed her lead. But then, in May 1771, the *Gospel Magazine*, the mouthpiece of Calvinistic Methodism, published the text of the Minutes, and in so doing raised the profile of the whole affair. A strategy of some kind became necessary to spearhead opposition to Wesley's views. Lady Huntingdon held a meeting with Walter Shirley, Richard Hill and two other laymen, Thomas Powys and James Ireland. They came up with the idea of a circular inviting all who opposed the theology of the Minutes to join them in a deputation to Wesley's next conference. Whether this was the brain-child of Lady Huntingdon and Shirley, which they then imposed on the others – or the other way round – is not clear. Each sought to shift responsibility onto the others when the circular received a distinctly cool response, even among some firm Calvinists. The notion of an uninvited deputation seemed to challenge the standards of gentlemanly conduct that were deemed to exist even between those separated by the deepest theological divides. Charles Wesley (despite not being entirely happy with the language of the Minutes) reacted angrily when Lady Huntingdon sent him a copy of the circular. He saw it as an attempt by her to drive a wedge between him and John, and wrote on her letter, 'Lady Huntingdon's LAST, UNANSWERED BY JOHN WESLEY'S BROTHER.'

Shirley and Lady Huntingdon recognized that they had gone too far, and they apologized to Wesley for appearing to challenge his authority. The result was an invitation to Shirley to attend Wesley's conference, and he did so with a small party of clergy and laymen. Perhaps wisely, Lady Huntingdon was not included in the delegation. The outcome was as good as one could have been expected in the circumstances: a declaration signed by the Wesleyans to the effect that the Minutes did not advocate justification by works, and a signed acknowledgement by Shirley that he had been wrong to think that they did. (Wesley's position, as he had argued to Lady Huntingdon a few weeks earlier, was that the Minutes did not imply a role for works in securing man's initial step on the path to salvation. Rather, they were concerned with the subsequent stages in the Christian life: 'not ... the condition of obtaining, but of continuing in the favour of God'.)

This might have marked the start of a period of reflection and healing. But Wesley promptly published a defence of the Minutes that Fletcher had prepared after leaving Trevecca. Fletcher argued that the Minutes were fully compatible with belief in man's sole dependence on Christ for salvation. In other words, Fletcher was saying nothing incompatible with the declaration that Wesley had just signed. But Wesley's decision to publish an extended justification of the Minutes, just at this precise moment, was all that was needed to keep the controversy alive. It seemed to imply that the Minutes had emerged unscathed from the debate with the Calvinists. Some commentators even said that the affair was a defeat for Lady Huntingdon and her circle. The response was a published *Narrative* of the events surrounding the conference, written by Shirley, but with an introduction and conclusion supplied by Lady Huntingdon. The production of such a document inevitably left the impression that its authors remained doubtful both of the Minutes' theology and of Wesley's integrity in defending them.

Shirley's *Narrative* functioned as a summary of the Connexion's doctrinal position, and it was widely distributed. It gave the Connexion a certain kudos, as a leading voice among the Calvinistic Methodists, and it went into a second edition in 1772, in reply to a further publication by Fletcher. This marked the effective end of the Connexion's role in the controversy, although it was not the end of the controversy itself. The fires that had been kindled by the Minutes, and Lady Huntingdon's response to them, burned for a while longer. On the Wesleyan side Fletcher kept up a steady stream of defences of Wesley and the Arminian position, producing in all six so-called *Checks to Antinomianism* between 1771 and 1775. The title demonstrates where Fletcher, like Wesley, thought that the real danger of Calvinism lay. Their fear was that it would lead to antinomianism – to the idea that the believer, being saved by grace, is freed from the constraints of the moral law. Their opponents, of course, denied that their system had this effect: good behaviour might not be necessary to attain salvation, but it was still vital evidence that one had in fact been saved.

The tone of the debate grew decidedly nasty. Late in 1771 Richard Hill published an account of a conversation that he and Martin Madan had in Paris with the head of a house of English Benedictines. They had shown the priest Wesley's Minutes and were delighted when he condemned them for placing too much emphasis on human righteousness, rather than the saving work of Christ. This was evidence, said Hill (showing little respect for their Parisian host), that the Minutes were 'too rotten even for a Papist to rest upon'. Hill's pamphlet went on to poke fun at Wesley's matrimonial problems, and included a 'paraphrase' of the declaration that Wesley had signed with Shirley:

Be it known from henceforth,
To each friend and each brother,
Whene'er we *say* one thing,
We *mean* quite *another*.

The Arminian side was not above personal abuse either. Wesley's associate Thomas Olivers (although himself denigrated by Richard Hill as 'a journeyman cordwainer') sneered at the student James Glazebrook's mining background, calling him 'a novice just come out of the coal pits'. The ironic titles of some of the pamphlets issued from the two sides over the following years give a flavour of the crude level at which the controversy was carried on:

Logica Wesleinsis; or The Farago double distilled, with an heroic poem in praise of John Wesley.

Sir Richard Hill, 1773.

The Christian World unmasked. Pray come and peep.

John Berridge, 1773.

Imposture detected & the dead [i.e., Whitefield] vindicated, in a letter . . . containing strictures on the false and libellous harangue lately delivered by Mr J Wesley . . .

Rowland Hill, 1777.

A rod for the reviler; or A full answer to Mr Rowland Hill's letter, entitled 'Imposture detected'.

Thomas Olivers, 1777.

While these vitriolic exchanges were going on, there was a measure of reconciliation between Lady Huntingdon and the leading Arminians. She resumed personal contact with Charles Wesley in the winter of 1772–73, and in 1775 was concerned to hear that John Wesley was seriously ill. This extract from her letter to Charles (and his careful draft of a reply) show the strength of the bonds that still existed between them – but also the need they both felt to tread warily with one another:

The relentings of every Christian affection engage me to enquire after my old friend your Brother, who I heard this day (& not before) is so ill. Not being well myself, the hearing of his danger has affected me very much . . . I do grieve to think his faithful labours are to cease yet on earth. How does an hour of loving sorrow swallow up the *just* differences our various Judgements make . . . I have loved him this five and thirty years & it is with pleasure I find he remains in my heart as a friend & a laborious beloved servant of Jesus Christ.

I deferred acknowledging your Ladyship's favour in hopes of sending you better news; but every letter ... calls us to give up our friend. We expect to hear by the next that he has finished his course. The work of all three [of us] is nearly finished. We shall be *in our death not divided*.

Lady Huntingdon to Charles Wesley, 28 June 1775 and Charles Wesley's draft of his reply, 2 July 1775. Meth. Arch. CHV 81.

It took longer for friendly relations to be restored between Lady Huntingdon and John Fletcher – indeed, in 1773 he lamented that 'With some people we must be *very near*, or *quite off*. I doubt whether this is not a little the case with our Great Friend.' It was his serious illness that proved the catalyst for renewed contacts in 1777, and he remained on cordial terms with members of Lady Huntingdon's circle until his death in 1785.

The personal relationship between Lady Huntingdon and John Wesley remained broadly harmonious for the remainder of their lives, and they treated each other with cautious respect. (They both died in 1791.) The Connexion did not take any further active part in the continuing doctrinal controversy. Indeed, Lady Huntingdon was upset by the virulent tone that was adopted by Rowland Hill in his 1777 attack on Wesley. This did not mean, however, that things went back to how they had been prior to 1770. The controversy had hardened Lady Huntingdon's attitude to non-Calvinist beliefs, alerting her to dangers that she had not previously suspected. At Trevecca, for example, she had previously tolerated Arminian sympathies on the part of teachers, and possibly some students. Now the college became solidly Calvinist. This limited its potential to serve the wider evangelical movement, though it is impossible to say how 'catholic' an institution it might otherwise have become. The most serious effect of the controversy upon the college was the loss of Fletcher's leadership, since no-one of comparable spiritual stature was to work at Trevecca again. It also seems that the Connexion became more self-consciously Calvinist after 1770, with provisions appearing in chapel trust deeds restricting pulpits to preachers of approved orthodoxy.

The Connexion's period of expansion was only just getting under way when the controversy broke out in 1770. This makes it difficult to judge how far the pattern of expansion was affected by the dispute. Did Lady Huntingdon consciously seek to evangelize areas that were already served by Wesley's preachers? Certainly Wesley thought that she was guilty of precisely that. In 1776, for example, he challenged her with threatening his activities in Cornwall. Her reply was that there was plenty of work there for both connexions, which was a fair point. But she also argued that since their doctrines were so different, people should be given a choice – which does imply that she thought it reasonable for both groups to operate in the same area. She claimed to have forbidden her students from making personal attacks on Wesley or his preachers. Nevertheless, over the following years Wesley's *Journal* contains a series of complaints about their activities. In 1779, for example:

> I reached Grimsby, and found a little trial. In this, and many other parts of the kingdom, those striplings who call themselves Lady Huntingdon's preachers have greatly hindered the work of God. They have neither sense, courage, nor grace to go and beat up the devil's quarters in any place where Christ has not been named; but wherever we have entered as by storm, and gathered a few souls, often at the peril of our lives, they creep in, and, by doubtful disputations, set everyone's sword against his brother. One of these has just crept into Grimsby, and is striving to divide the poor little flock.
>
> John Wesley's *Journal* for 3 July 1779. *Works*, xxiii, 138.

Local rivalry between Lady Huntingdon's Connexion and Wesley's Methodists worked both ways, and there are many examples of her congregations feeling threatened by Wesleyans. Congregations would complain to Lady Huntingdon that Wesley had, for example, built a new meeting-house in the area, or had taken to sending his best preachers there – so she had better provide them with a reliable supply of competent ministers, or Connexion members would defect to the Wesleyans. Such fears might be related to doctrinal factors, with worshippers being enticed in one direction or the other by the superior claims of Calvinism or Arminianism. It is certainly apparent, from the reports that occasionally reached Lady Huntingdon of clashes between congregations and their ministers, that some of the Connexion's adherents thought seriously about the theological matters that we have been considering in this chapter. Most people were probably indifferent to the ideological issues that had split the Revival, however, and were influenced by more basic considerations – like whether they could rely on the regularity of services, or the skill of preachers. As usual, it often came down to money. If a chapel lost members to a more attractive rival, its income would probably be reduced – and that would threaten its ability to stay open.

Interestingly, some other groups of Calvinist evangelicals also came to be regarded as a threat to the Connexion. This underlined the fact that it was not only theology that could lead to conflict: rivalry and competition at local level could be just as important. The most significant of these other Calvinist groups was the network of congregations that had been founded by George Whitefield, the so-called 'Tabernacle Connexion'. Whitefield might well have decided to entrust his congregations to Lady Huntingdon's care at his death in 1770, just as he did with his work in America (see chapter 13). In fact the bulk of the congregations passed into the care of trustees – two London laymen, Keen and West. In Gloucestershire, however, Whitefield's societies formed a separate entity, known as the 'Rodborough Connexion'; these came under the effective oversight of Rowland Hill.

The initial period after Whitefield's death was a time of close collaboration between the Tabernacle Connexion and Lady Huntingdon. There are instances, over the next three or four years, of her sending students to serve at their chapels, and on at least one occasion she used the house attached to the Moorfields Tabernacle as a place to stay while she was visiting London. It was in 1776 that signs of strain first appeared. The cause seems to have been Lady Huntingdon's suspicion that Rowland Hill was encroaching upon her work at Haverfordwest, and also that the Rodborough Connexion was planning to have some of her students ordained without her consent. Lady Huntingdon reacted emotionally to these supposed threats to her work, much as she had to the Wesleyan Minutes. She even had to be dissuaded by some of her clergy friends from bringing a complaint about the matter before the Anglican bishops – an extraordinary idea, when one thinks how little respect her own activities showed for the rules of the Church:

> I must own I should hesitate much before I should bring complaints against those that hold the truth before a Bench of corrupt ungodly men. I feel the justest resentment & indignation at the act of ordaining of your Ladyship's students without your ... consent ... But still permit me to observe to my noble friend that the offence is rather against a Connexion, than against the truth & the general interest of Christ's kingdom ... After remonstrating to the parties & the connexion where our noble Patroness has received such base & unworthy treatment, we [should] withdraw ourselves & our services, & accordingly I neither have nor will preach either at Tottenham [Court Road] or the Tabernacle till your Ladyship has received full satisfaction.

> Walter Shirley to Lady Huntingdon, 14 November 1776. F1/1734, CF.

Once Lady Huntingdon's suspicions were aroused, however, they were not easily dispelled. Other actions by the Tabernacle trustees were interpreted by her as attempts to muscle in on her work, and the breach widened. Over the following years there were several instances of rivalry between individual chapels of the two connexions. And the chapter of accidents that surrounded her work in America, as we shall see, also soured relations with the Tabernacle trustees. Though there were some attempts at reunion during the 1780s, these came to nothing. To the end of Lady Huntingdon's life, the two connexions continued their suspicious separate existence.

As we have seen, Rowland Hill – once a young protégé of Lady Huntingdon – had first incurred her displeasure through his association with the Tabernacle Connexion. He was soon to be regarded as a danger in his own right, suspected of wanting to found a connexion of his own. As ever, the perceived crime was appearing to trespass upon her work. Lady Huntingdon refused his requests to be reconciled with her, and in her will forbade him from preaching in any of her pulpits. (He was not the only minister to be black-balled in this way.) Hill was to become one of a number of free-floating Calvinist evangelicals – operating on their own or in small groups – that appeared in the latter part of the eighteenth century. For the most part they co-existed peacefully alongside Lady Huntingdon's Connexion, though there was always the fear of rivalry. This was even true of one other group that we have not mentioned before: the small connexion of churches founded by Lady Huntingdon's Scottish friend (and in a sense counterpart) Willielma Campbell, Viscountess Glenorchy. Lady Glenorchy's work was mostly in Scotland, but she opened a few chapels in England, particularly in the south-west. There was no reason at all why this development should have impinged on Lady Huntingdon. But such was her paranoia that it was still necessary for friends to assure her that there was no threat.

The Calvinistic Controversy raised theological questions that seemed central to evangelicals at the time – even though there was no way they could ever be satisfactorily answered. Lady Huntingdon's Connexion happened to be the first to spot the significance of Wesley's 1770 Minutes, and for a while it became the standard-bearer of Calvinist orthodoxy. Other, more extreme, exponents soon emerged. The Connexion was not entirely free from extreme Calvinists, as we shall see in the final chapter. And there were cases of antinomianism among some of the students – instances of (particularly sexual) licence, justified by the young men on the grounds that, as part of the elect, they were above the moral law. To the extent that it is possible to speak of a 'Connexion theology', however, it was at the moderate end of the Calvinist spectrum. That is to say, its leaders were generally happier talking about God's grace to the elect, rather than dwelling on the fate of the damned. But theology, as we have seen, was not necessarily the most important consideration in determining whether evangelicals cooperated with each other, or found themselves in competition.

Perhaps the biggest impact that the controversy had upon the Connexion was in respect of Trevecca, which it deprived of Fletcher's inspiring leadership. We shall shortly return to the college, to consider what it was like during the remainder of Lady Huntingdon's life. But first we need to look at the other important development that began in 1770.

13

America: Bethesda Orphan House and Academy

※❦❧❀

The news of George Whitefield's death reached Lady Huntingdon in November 1770. It was a severe personal blow, and it deprived her of the one major figure in the Revival whom she held in unreserved respect. It also, as she subsequently learned, brought her possession of the orphanage that Whitefield had founded at Bethesda, near Savannah in Georgia. Whitefield's bequest was to have a profound impact on Lady Huntingdon, and its effects were to be felt for the rest of her life. She was to pass, in a short time, from thinking Bethesda her greatest opportunity, to regarding it as her worst disaster:

> This opening in America is the astonishment of all that love or fear the Lord . . .
>
> Lady Huntingdon to John Hawksworth, 10 September 1772. G2/1/3, CF.

> The Lord has caused dear Mr Whitefield to suffer much through this place & indeed myself much more . . . No trials thro my life have been equal to these.
>
> Lady Huntingdon to James Habersham, 28 July 1773. A3/15/2A, CF.

The idea of an orphanage in Georgia came initially from the young colony's board of trustees, back in the 1730s. Whitefield responded to their initiative, and had started planning for the project before his first voyage to Georgia in 1738. The orphanage received a grant of some 500 acres by the Georgia trustees, and there were 40 orphans by the time building work began in 1740. It was originally envisaged that the children would engage in cotton-picking and spinning, alongside their studies, in order to make the institution self-financing. Despite this, the place seems to have been plagued by financial difficulties for most of its existence. Slavery had been outlawed in Georgia since the colony was first founded, but Whitefield soon decided that slaves were essential for the financial viability of his orphanage – so he added his support to that of other pro-slavery Georgians, who secured a change in the colony's law in 1750. Whitefield's plan was to generate income by growing rice. Over the years he built up his slave- and land-holding, so that he bequeathed to Lady Huntingdon some 50 slaves and nearly 5,000 acres – but also substantial debts, because even this new approach failed to make the Orphan House pay its way. In fact, by the time of his death Whitefield had radically changed his mind about the purpose of the institution, and was seeking legislative authority from the Assembly of Georgia to turn it into a college or academy.

Several options were open to Lady Huntingdon. Most obviously she could have declined the bequest and relinquished the estate back to the province. Alternatively, she could have followed up Whitefield's idea of creating some sort of academic institution. Or she could even have continued with an orphanage – which was, after all, the purpose for which the place had been founded, and for which donations had originally been sought. Surprisingly, she seems to have given little thought to the interests of the orphans. Nor did she seem concerned at the morality of keeping slaves. Like the Bible – but unlike John Wesley and many evangelicals of a younger generation – she accepted slavery as a fact, and contented herself with hoping that the slaves concerned would gain spiritually from having Christian owners. She remained unmoved in 1774 when the Quaker philanthropist Anthony Benezet sought to enlist her support for abolition. It is difficult to know what was in her mind when she asked for a female slave to be purchased for Bethesda, and named Selina after her.

Lady Huntingdon was not attracted to Whitefield's idea of a secular academy. She decided instead to turn her bequest into a college that would be the base for a missionary initiative in North America. Such an undertaking would embrace the Indian nations, as well as colonists. As described in a subsequent pamphlet, her ambitions were all-embracing: her 'intention was to carry into execution that which she believed would most effectively be the means of promoting the knowledge of Christ, in the various provinces of America'. It is not difficult to see why she thought that Bethesda could be used in this way. The Orphan House came into her possession little more than two years after the founding of Trevecca, which had provided a dramatic demonstration of how a college could be used as a basis for itinerant evangelism. Added to that was her long-standing interest in foreign missions. This can be traced right back to the 1740s, and she had recently had some first-hand involvement in overseas work. This was in 1769, when she agreed to a request to send two Trevecca students to help with a scheme to found a Protestant settlement on the East Indies island of Bencoolen. A further, less honourable, motive for the Bethesda venture may have been to challenge Wesley's influence in America. Some of Wesley's followers certainly suspected that this was the case.

There were two major factors that Lady Huntingdon failed to take into account, however. The first was the strength of Dissenting influence in Georgia, and the extent to which Dissenters had contributed to the funding of Bethesda. Lady Huntingdon's loyalty to the Church of England may have looked quite tenuous in England, but things appeared rather differently in Georgia. There was to be substantial local unhappiness about an English countess turning Bethesda into a centre for (apparently) extending the influence of the Anglican Church. The other factor was the sheer practical difficulty of supervising such an enterprise on the other side of the Atlantic, especially when the estate upon which it was to be based was one into which she had had no prior input. As we have seen, Lady Huntingdon ran her Connexion and Trevecca in an intensely personal way – and even then there were mistakes and misunderstandings. Now she was to be reliant on others (not to mention the vagaries of the trans-Atlantic post) to provide her with information about what individuals were doing, as well as the state of buildings and finances. Those informants often had their own interests and records to defend, so she could seldom be sure where the truth lay. At times she even considered going over to Bethesda herself. That might have made some difference – had her health stood up to the voyage – but it is doubtful whether even her indomitable presence could have made a success of the venture.

Lady Huntingdon's original idea was to send over a group of ordained students, and in the spring of 1771 she approached the Bishop of London to this end. The Bishop had earlier agreed to ordain one (but not both) of the students who went to Bencoolen, but this time he was more cautious. He was worried about treading on the toes of the Society for the Propagation of the Gospel, which had overall charge of missionary activity in the colony. The most he would agree to do was ordain a chaplain to the Orphan House, and then only on condition that the man concerned would agree not to become an itinerant evangelist. Lady Huntingdon claimed that she could find no-one willing to be restricted in this way. More likely it was she who was not prepared to give up her American ambitions. Accordingly she changed tack, and decided to find an existing clergyman who would head a team that consisted of an ordained schoolmaster and a group of students. Finding a suitable leader proved difficult, but Lady Huntingdon eventually settled on the Revd William Piercy. Piercy was an interesting example of a Calvinist evangelical clergyman of the period. He had served at the Lock Hospital (and had been dismissed from there because of his outdoor preaching), and had preached both for the Tabernacle and Countess Connexions. His main sphere of activity was now a chapel at Woolwich that had been built for him, and to which Lady Huntingdon was to provide financial help. He was still under 30. It was intended that he should be accompanied by his brother Richard; another clergyman, the Revd Charles Stuart Eccles, as schoolmaster; eight students; and the Trevecca housekeeper Betty Hughes.

The planning stretched through 1771 and into the following year. In the summer of 1772 Lady Huntingdon sent instructions that the remaining orphans should be moved out of the orphanage, and in October she called a great meeting at Trevecca to inaugurate the mission. It was an occasion of high hopes and high drama. When Lady Huntingdon and her accompanying clergymen arrived at Trevecca, they were escorted into the college by hymn-singing students, who continued their serenade while she had dinner. During the coming week over 30 sermons were preached, both by clergy and students. Those students who had volunteered for America were examined as to their calling, and Lady Huntingdon made clear that her good opinion did not depend upon their going: 'her kindest care and protection would alike at all times be over those who stayed, as well as those who went'. Then came the actual day of commissioning, starting (as had each day of the past week) with a Communion service:

> The students to be devoted to God for the work in America stood in front of the table, and after the Communion-service was read, and the elements consecrated, Mr Piercy addressed himself . . . to the students . . . He laid before them in the strongest manner possible, the trials, temptations, dangers and hardships . . . they must expect to meet with . . . and earnestly exhorted them before they devoted themselves at his table, and there sealed themselves his servants for those particular purposes, that they would examine their hearts, as in the presence

of God; and that if there were any conscious reserves there, any drawing back from the Lord, or the calls they had professed, or that any among them was fearful or faint-hearted, begged they would withdraw.

Some Account of the Proceedings at the College of the Right Hon. The Countess of Huntingdon, in Wales, Relative to those Students called to go to her Ladyship's College in Georgia . . ., London, 1772.

None of them did withdraw, in the face of this emotional pressure. (Had they realized that their greatest 'trials and hardships' would come from Piercy himself, they might well have decided differently.)

The Trevecca commissioning was followed by further, similar services at Whitefield's former chapels in London. But thereafter it was downhill all the way. One of the students developed small-pox, prior to departure; most of the students were left behind when their ship sailed unexpectedly; and one of the eight never made it to America at all. Two students, Joseph Cook and John Cosson, together with the housekeeper Betty Hughes, reached the Orphan House in January 1773. They found it in a markedly worse state than expected:

There is neither mutton, veal, eggs, cheese, or fowls in the house, or money to buy any . . . The students' rooms are not near done, and it will amount to £200 to make them complete. The dwelling-house is likewise very much out of repair.

When I first saw this place my heart greatly sunk to see such a delightful place in such a situation – no individual thing in the garden, though things will grow all the year round; no fowls or furniture in the house, not even sheeting . . . I am told the house is now in debt £350 and I am sure £500 more would not furnish and repair it properly.

Letters to Lady Huntingdon from Cook and Cosson, 8 & 9 January 1773. A3/4(8) & (3), CF.

There were to be claims and counter-claims about who had brought the place to this state. The only brighter news was that John Cosson and Betty Hughes had been married as soon as they reached Georgia. It was a different story, four months later, when Betty gave birth. The couple claimed that they had been married secretly (by a layman) the previous year, but that did not prevent Cosson being sent back to England in disgrace. Although she was upset by the Cossons' deception, Lady Huntingdon was less shocked by this incident than might have been expected. Cosson was in due course restored to her favour and, at her expense, to his wife and child in America (Betty died during a further pregnancy in 1776.) Perhaps Lady Huntingdon's Calvinist theology made her relaxed about human frailty. Or perhaps she empathized with her errant student, as she thought back fondly to the passion of her own marriage.

William Piercy had been the last of the expedition to reach Bethesda, in March 1773. But with his arrival began a fresh phase in the traumas of the Orphan House. Before he left England Lady Huntingdon had spoken of him as a successor to Whitefield – a description that seems to have fitted closely with Piercy's own estimation of his calling and abilities. From the start the students had grumbled about each other to Lady Huntingdon. Very soon Piercy was also criticizing their motivation and worldliness. They in turn sent her a catalogue of complaints about his ill-treatment of them, and his arrogance, pomposity and extravagance. Other people commented on some of the same traits: there is a memorable description of Piercy 'going through the continent with his phaeton and pair of fine horses, with his black boy to fan him in the pulpit while he was preaching, and all at the expense of Lady Huntingdon'. (A later report to Lady Huntingdon by Richard Piercy was if anything worse: in his account it was a phaeton and *four* horses, and he used a student to drive him.)

One respect in which Piercy certainly differed from Whitefield was his lack of respect for Dissenters. This further strengthened local resentment at the perceived Anglican take-over of the Orphan House. An article highly critical of the new regime, and the attitude being taken to Dissenters, appeared in the *Georgia Gazette* at the end of May 1773. Three days later a fire – which may well have been deliberate – destroyed Bethesda's main buildings and their contents.

The fire was the final straw for some of the students. It confirmed their sense that they would achieve nothing in America. That feeling was compounded by the domineering attitude of Piercy, who was reluctant to allow them to preach outside the estate. The letters they wrote to Lady Huntingdon in this period give an insight into the bond that existed between them and their patroness. They told her frankly of their problems with Piercy and of their feelings for her. 'I love [you] next to my own Mother,' said one. Her letters to Piercy reveal how far she reciprocated those feelings: she could mother her dependent students in a way that had often proved impossible with her own children. Her letters also show how close she came to giving up the whole American venture, and how desperate she was at the spiralling costs it entailed:

> My present distress is such that you cannot refuse seeing me as soon as possible. I have this day accepted the bills on account of your being . . . abroad, but alas so large a sum I have no one to help in & so short a time to raise it . . . If needful I will return with you, but one single shilling I cannot advance at present save the draft of one hundred pounds to bring you over . . . Request the dear students to stay only till your return.

> The students . . . are far from happy, and unless a spirit of love & tenderness rules over them, they will find their way back to me. They complain of bondage and are not at sufficient liberty . . . They have been used by me so kindly that they will not bear an unnecessary servility.

... the mutual complaints on both sides must make me think faults on both sides. However I see no way but having it in their power to return.

Lady Huntingdon to William Piercy, 11 August, 22 September & 6 October 1773. A4/3(1), (2A) & (3), CF.

Piercy, however, was not for giving up the opportunities that America offered him, and he clearly regarded her purse as bottomless. In the very first letter he wrote her after the fire – estimated rebuilding cost two thousand pounds, with only a few hundred promised locally – he presented her with a shopping list of other items including 'two dozen of fine shirts for travelling & one dozen of cambric stocks . . . I should also be glad of a cask of red wine . . .' Piercy did not return to England, as she had asked, but over the following months persuaded her not to give up the trust that she had inherited from Whitefield. He sent her enticing accounts of the opportunities open to them, passing on the view of one influential local sympathizer that once they started preaching in the back settlements 'we shall instantly have several churches built upon our own Plan which will rest in our entire Possession as in England'. By early 1774 he had also convinced her that the estate could be made self-sufficient, by growing rice for sale in London. An American visitor to England advised her that this was probably a correct assessment, though he passed on the received wisdom among planters that, when an estate owner was at a distance, it was better to sell up and invest the money. She ignored this sensible advice, as well as the chilling comment that slaves' productivity was less with rice than sugar, because of the unhealthiness of the crop: 'sometimes almost all the working Negroes are swept off by fevers in a season, and the Planters obliged entirely to renew the Stock'.

The estate probably did meet its running costs over the next few years, though it never repaid Lady Huntingdon's immense capital outlay. The surviving accounts suggest that nearly £3,000 had gone on the initial expedition; another £3,500 were to be spent over the period up to late 1775, including £2,000 on fresh slaves. While Lady Huntingdon was thus being persuaded to go on underwriting Bethesda – and with it, Piercy's continuing dream of being a second Whitefield in America – the students got on with pursuing their own vocations, where and however they could. All left the Orphan House over the following years, most finding ministerial positions among the Dissenters. With one exception, Lady Huntingdon sent no more students to Bethesda during the 1770s. The exception was a black student, David Margate, who accompanied Cosson on his return to America in 1774. This may have been a belated attempt by Lady Huntingdon to address the spiritual needs of the Orphan House slaves, but the attempt back-fired badly. It had been naïve of Lady Huntingdon not to have anticipated that a black preacher – himself a former slave – would encounter hostility in a society of white slave-owners. So we have to allow for the possibility of bias in the reports that she received about him. These were that Margate had caused offence to colonists in South Carolina, by remarks made in the course of a lecture. Worse, he had gone on to proclaim himself a second Moses and to preach insurrection among slaves there and in Georgia. There were also allegations of inappropriate behaviour with women slaves. Whatever the truth of these reports, Piercy showed a staggering lack of understanding of how someone in Margate's position must have felt when confronted again with the institution of slavery:

> His pride seems so great that he can't bear to think of any of his own colour being slaves – though he has confessed that he was a runaway slave himself.

> Piercy to Lady Huntingdon (probably April 1775). A4/2(16C), CF.

Matters came to a head in May 1775 with reports that a lynch mob had set out from South Carolina, determined to hang him.

Margate was hastily shipped out of America for his own safety.

The backdrop to the Margate saga was the growing tension between the American colonies and the British Crown that led to the War of Independence. This had potentially serious implications for Lady Huntingdon's American interests, and for a period between 1775 and 1777 she lost all contact with Bethesda. Piercy himself had come out in support of what he described to Lady Huntingdon as the 'poor oppressed Provincials'. This may have protected Bethesda from the worst effects of the troubles. In October 1777, when he found a way of getting a letter back to England, he reported that their only loss had been three slaves taken by loyalists – though the estate's income had been undermined by a drastic fall in the price of rice. Bethesda's prospects worsened considerably the following year, after Georgia was recaptured by British forces. According to Piercy's later account, property was taken from Bethesda by the British, and he himself was regarded as politically suspect. In 1779 he judged it prudent to leave Bethesda for South Carolina, but it was not till the following year that he received permission from the Carolina authorities to return to Europe. He reached Ireland early in 1781.

Lady Huntingdon had for a long time been uneasy about Piercy's reported extravagance and his failure to account for the money that passed through his hands. Now she was able to communicate her unease directly to Piercy – who, in return, displayed the spirit of aggrieved and ingratiating self-justification that was to mark his letters over the coming years. First he denied reports that he had been sympathetic to the colonists – evidently forgetting what he had said to Lady Huntingdon about them six years earlier. Then he professed his faithful stewardship at Bethesda, and his devotion to her:

What is my crime that has been any *procuring* cause of forfeiting your best esteem? Indeed my greatest crime has ever been, if it may be called criminal, loving you too much . . . I only continued in America to serve you ... You ever had & ever will have in me a son, a servant, a friend, without art, without interest, & without guile.

...the great caution and reserve manifest in your letter is too, too pungent for the feelings of my love & eternal friendship to you to bear, but sure I am you judge you have just ground thus to act ...

P.S. I have just received information ... that I am charged as the greatest villain as having drawn on you for enormous sums which are squandered away by me & never accounted for.

All the many sore, grievous & unheard of trials & opposition I have met with for nine years past are nothing ... when compared with this last of all from you ... God knoweth that my wife, my babies, my nearest friends were all as nothing when compared with this sacred and divine friendship [with you].

Piercy to Lady Huntingdon, 15 & 20 January & 8 February 1781.
A4/2(21A), (22A) & (22C), A4/6(4), CF.

Piercy was initially able to persuade Lady Huntingdon of his innocence. For a while he resumed ministry in the Connexion, including taking part in 1781 in an extended preaching tour with Wills and Glascott, of which a report was published the following year. Subsequently he resumed preaching at his old chapel at Woolwich. His relations with Lady Huntingdon became tense again during 1782. As we shall see in the next chapter, Lady Huntingdon was by that time embroiled in a battle with the church authorities that was about to culminate in her secession from the Church of England. If she were to operate her Connexion effectively outside the Church, she needed a cadre of clergymen who would join her in seceding. She identified a number of men who she thought should take this step, and worked hard to persuade them – and was characteristically outraged when most refused. Piercy was one of them.

Even that did not terminate their relationship, but the end came in the summer of 1783. The breach was down to a mix of factors: Lady Huntingdon's suspicion that Piercy had designs on her Bath chapel; business advice she had received on the unsatisfactory state of the Bethesda accounts; and Piercy's claim (which he now made for the first time) that she owed him years of back pay for the time he had spent in America. It was agreed to submit the last two issues to arbitration. Piercy nominated Keen (a trustee of the Tabernacle Connexion) as one of his assessors – a decision that was to lead to a final breach between Lady Huntingdon and Keen. Lady Huntingdon charged Piercy with major financial irregularities. We do not know how much help she received in formulating her case, but she certainly took a close interest in the details. The following extracts give a flavour of the list of 30 'queries' that were put to the assessors on Lady Huntingdon's behalf:

8. Did Lady Huntingdon ever receive a voucher [receipt] for any one payment ever made by Mr Piercy abroad, or does she now know if a single debt of Mr Whitefield's was paid for which Mr Piercy's draft of £1000 was accepted?
9. Did Lady Huntingdon, or did she not, mention to Mr Piercy his choice of a salary, did she not request & even press him to name it, & did he or did he not avoid it?
13. Did Mr Piercy, or did he not, ever send over one shilling from the estate in eight years on any occasion, or even a barrel of rice, or the smallest acknowledgement from her property under him?
14. Did it ever appear, or did it not, that in eight years a poor orphan was ever taught to read, or a morsel of bread or clothing given to the poor out of her whole estate, which after the year 1774 had him only to maintain, the students being all gone?
16. & 17. Did he, or did he not, ever consult Lady Huntingdon in purchase or sale of her slaves? Did he, or did he not, ever

send Lady Huntingdon a list of those slaves bought with her
money...?
19. Did she ever know her property was disposed of till the
merchants in England first was informed of it?

'Queries for Mr Piercy'. A4/4(6A) & (6B), CF.

Piercy, by contrast, argued that he had never been Lady
Huntingdon's agent for Bethesda (so none of this was anything to do with him) and that the sole issue for the assessors
was how much *he* was owed. The atmosphere between them
became increasingly bitter. In January 1784 he quoted back to
Lady Huntingdon extracts from her earlier letters that appeared
to commit her to a generous settlement – and threatened to publish them if satisfactory payment were not made. She was not a
woman to be cowed by such tactics: she described him soon after
as 'a character the most corrupt for ten years past'.

So far as we can tell, the case was never resolved in Britain,
although Piercy revived his claims against the then trustees of
Bethesda College, after he had moved back to America in 1796.
Whatever the truth of his stewardship of the Orphan House, the
allegations seem to have done his reputation no harm on that side
of the Atlantic: Piercy ended his career as rector of an Episcopal
church in South Carolina.

The dispute with Piercy was the sad culmination of the initiative that had started with so many sermons and high hopes at
Trevecca, back in 1772. But it did not mean that Lady Huntingdon
had given up interest in America. From 1782 she sought to ini-
tiate a scheme to found settlements of evangelical artisans in
various parts of the country. The idea was that their example
would be the means of civilizing and evangelizing the Indian
nations. Lady Huntingdon even contemplated going to America
herself to promote the project – which was pretty brave, in that
period, for a woman who was already in her mid-70s. In fact she
sought to interest George Washington, to whom she claimed to

be distantly related. Washington was respectful and friendly, and offered 'general superintendence or incidental attention', but he declined to take any direct part. In the event Lady Huntingdon's scheme foundered on the reluctance of the States in question to allocate the land necessary for the proposed settlements.

Apart from these new plans, there was still the fate of Bethesda to be resolved. She had had no news about the state of her American property for some years, and in 1783 gave power of attorney to Henry Laurens, an American about to return to South Carolina. Laurens's own estates had suffered badly from the troubles, however. In 1785 he was still dealing with his own problems, and could not promise Lady Huntingdon when he might make it to Georgia. The following year another solution presented itself, when the State General Assembly proposed turning the Orphan House into the University of Georgia. Lady Huntingdon was not enthusiastic about the idea, because she still hoped that Whitefield's bequest could be used to support missionary work among native Americans. Her reply to the university trustees was made to sound more positive, however, but it was subject to one fundamental objection:

Lady Huntingdon ... considers herself much obliged by the information [the Trustees] have been so good to give her of their having entered upon so noble a plan of usefulness ... Its most prosperous successes, both religiously & civily, will ever stand nearly connected with her happiness, it having been long an object of her wishes that such an important event might [take] place ... It is her desire therefore to have no reserves on a subject of such consequence to her very much honoured & respected friends ... [So] she takes the liberty to enquire certainly if she is mistaken in the Ninth and Eleventh articles of the Charter ('that all professions of Christianity are alike to be established') a latitude which may infer in the end that even Popish bishops and tutors may become the guardians of the youth and their instructors. This as it appears to Lady Huntingdon must sooner or later end in the most wretched slavery both in Church and State.

Lady Huntingdon to the Trustees of the University of Georgia, 15 January 1787. A3/12(10), CF.

She was clearly in two minds about the proposal, as she even offered the trustees the drawings she had had made (but not used) for a new college in Wales when the Trevecca lease ran out. The legal advice that she subsequently received in England, however, was that a secular university like this would run counter to the terms of Whitefield's will. In the event, nothing more was heard of the university proposal during Lady Huntingdon's lifetime.

Bethesda clearly haunted her, however. It represented a solemn trust that she had not been able to honour. So she continued with attempts to sort out its affairs. In 1788 she sent over a student called David Phillips, though the only result of his trip was to reveal the extent to which the estate was in debt. Then in 1790 she sent a further student, John Johnson. Touchingly (or obstinately) she clung to her old vision of using Bethesda to evangelize the Indians: Johnson, she said, 'goes to America for me, to labour to fulfil my long desired plan for the Indian Natives'. Reports of Lady Huntingdon's death reached Georgia before Johnson could make any moves in this direction. The news brought to a head local resentment at Bethesda's remaining in English hands, and by the end of 1791 an Act had been passed to establish Bethesda College. Early in January the College trustees appropriated the estate, and Johnson was briefly imprisoned for attempting to stop them. So the ill-fated saga of Lady Huntingdon's American possessions came to an end. For two decades – the most crowded years of Lady Huntingdon's life – Bethesda had cost her money, time and grief. It is doubtful whether the venture achieved any of the objectives which she had originally set for it.

Before we leave the theme of foreign missions, there are two other planned overseas ventures that should be briefly mentioned. The first also involved North America. This was an initiative in 1788 involving two students being sent to New Brunswick in Nova Scotia. Their expedition appears to have been rather better planned than previous ones: for one thing the two men were both ordained before they set out. But judging from a miserable letter received back from one of them in 1792, the outcome had been little more successful. The other stemmed from a vision not of Lady Huntingdon, but of Thomas Haweis, who came to play a decisive part in the Connexion at the end of her life. Haweis had long been excited by accounts of the Pacific, and he persuaded Lady Huntingdon to allow two further students to prepare to join an expedition to Tahiti. They were due to go early in 1791, so Lady Huntingdon would just have heard of their setting off before she died. The men refused, however, to go without Church of England ordination. This proved a sticking point that could not be got round, and they did not go. Given the track record of Trevecca students abroad, this may have been fortunate.

14

Life at Trevecca College

We left the story of Trevecca College after its foundation, and when Lady Huntingdon had started to use her students as preachers in the Connexion. We shall now look briefly at some of the main features of the college over the 23 years of its life in Wales.

A key question with any academic institution is who is in charge, and what is their style of leadership. Trevecca had got off to a good start under the presidency of John Fletcher. The adjective 'saintly' is often (and deservedly) applied to Fletcher, but that did not mean that he was a push-over where the students were concerned. We get some idea of the intellectual demands he made of his pupils from the work he set them during one of the times he was away. Only one of the items demanded a knowledge of Latin, but as it involved the students translating into that language the whole of the Church of England's thirty-nine doctrinal articles, it was a massive task for anyone without a solid classical education. The rest of the set exercises were in English, and were a test both of the students' theological understanding (for example, they had to explain how Christian baptism differed from that of John the Baptist) and of their ability to preach and defend the faith. They were required, for example, to draft a letter to a deist (that is, someone who denies that God reveals himself in the world), defending the truth of the Bible.

Fletcher was just as rigorous when it came to the students' religious lives. Within a few months of the college's foundation he lectured them on what he saw as their spiritual deadness, and threatened to ask Lady Huntingdon to expel all but the most devoted. His threat had the desired effect, for a mini-revival broke out across the whole college, involving the domestic staff as well as the students:

> When the afternoon lecture was over, I stayed in the study answering some questions . . . About half an hour after five Ellis came in a hurry to the study and said 'Hull and Cosson have got together and pray as I have never heard anybody pray' . . . I had taken the students that were in the study to the bottom of the stairs, from whence we could hear . . . when shame had covered their faces I took them to my room and began to pray also. By and by one and another of the students came [to join] us; about 8 o'clock our hearts were greatly enlarged . . . We were in the dark but we needed no candle, not so much as to give out hymns, admirably proper verses being given to one or another of the young men . . . Betty our maid had stole into the room . . . We prayed with and over her for about an hour more, when the Lord set her at liberty.
>
> . . . The next morning I was agreeably waked by the hymns & prayers of the young men.

Fletcher to Lady Huntingdon, 10 November 1768. F1/1449, CF.

Five days later the revival was still going on.

One of the tragedies of Trevecca was that leadership of the quality that Fletcher provided was available for only a short time. Fletcher's presidency, as we saw, was one of the victims of the quarrel between Lady Huntingdon and Wesley in the early 1770s. Fletcher resigned from Trevecca in March 1771; Joseph Benson, who provided much of the day-to-day teaching and who was also linked to Wesley, had already left. At times over the following years the students were effectively self-taught, under the supervision of one of their number as a kind of 'senior student'. This must have reduced the value of their college experience for all concerned. The names of other masters appear at various times, including two who were in post for significant periods. They were both Church of England clergymen, Samuel Phillips and later another John Williams, this one the son of the eminent Welsh preacher and hymn-writer, William Williams of Pantecelyn. Williams in particular struggled to raise the academic standards of his pupils, though he was often in despair:

> I am really ashamed to send out ... some of the young men that came here lately. Your Ladyship cannot therefore expect some of them out for a considerable time. 'Tis a great disgrace to the English nation that they bring up their children so. I have informed some of them of their faults about four, five, or six hundred times.

> We procured a horse last Saturday and sent one of the best young men we have here [to Hereford], who owing to his deficiency as a preacher drove almost all the congregation out ... The Hereford people say they would rather shut up the chapel than have any to serve them that are at college at present. Indeed the senior students that are here now are by far more stupid ... than any I ever had. I know not when they will be able with propriety to read a chapter of English properly.

John Williams to Lady Huntingdon, 21 February & 3 April 1788. F1/706, CF; D2538, 8/1, GRO.

Of course not all the students were as poor as that quote suggests. A great deal depended on their backgrounds, and the educational standards they had reached prior to admission. Some students had previously been clerks or apprentices; at least one had been a collier. Most had had some form of rudimentary education, and a few had undertaken private study, but their overall standard at admission seems to have been quite low. Another problem was that some students were native Welsh speakers, for whom preaching in English presented a further challenge. Most prospective students were interviewed prior to entry, but it seems likely that the main focus of such an examination was on the man's sense of vocation, rather than on his intellectual gifts.

A major factor militating against academic progress at Trevecca was the frequency with which study was interrupted by preaching missions. As we saw, this started early in the life of the college, and it soon became the norm for students to spend significant periods of time away. Most students probably welcomed this opportunity to try out their preaching skills for real. The experience must have been very different from the custom of giving trial sermons before the master and other students, which seems to have been a regular feature of Trevecca life. (Preaching to a congregation was possibly less nerve-wracking as well: one student was so scared of giving a college sermon that he could only get through by preaching with his back to the master and the other students!) Nevertheless students often complained to Lady Huntingdon about the effect that long absences on preaching tours had upon their studies and their future prospects. The following is a particularly frank example:

> I beg you be not angry with me in reminding you of your past promises to me respecting my coming to college last February, May, and August was twelve months [i.e., a year ago last February, May etc.] ... Three years almost I have been in your Ladyship's Connexion and have not been in college three months, whilst others have been there the greatest part of the time ... I am labouring and expending my time to no advantage as to this life ... If God should be pleased to gather you home to his blessed self, I must then despair of any opportunity to improve myself; although learning do not make ministers, it is necessary for ministers to have it.

Thomas Suter to Lady Huntingdon, 14 September 1782. E4/4(12), CF.

Because the students were out so much, it is impossible to say what was regarded as the normal length of a Trevecca 'course'. Three years was what Lady Huntingdon originally intended, but preaching commitments meant that no-one spent anything like this period of time actually at Trevecca. Three years probably represented the outside period that anyone was regarded as a student – though even this is largely guesswork, since it is impossible to say with certainty who counted as a student at any one time. On a very rough average, there would have been around eight to a dozen students resident at Trevecca at any one time, plus a dozen to fifteen itinerant preachers who were treated as students still linked to the college.

We have mentioned some of the teachers at Trevecca. But the greatest impact upon the students is likely to have come from Lady Huntingdon herself. She spent substantial periods of time at her college: between 1770 and 1787, she was there for more than eighty months in total – the equivalent of nearly seven years. She was not a distant presence while she was in residence. The huge number of letters she received from her students – many of them spontaneous and unaffected in the way they told her of their problems as well as their successes – is evidence of the bond she established with them. While she was at college, she would expound texts to the students, set them written exercises, and share her religious experience. The following passage comes from the autobiography of a former student, written nearly 50 years after the events in question. It vividly describes the concern she showed after he was taken ill while out preaching, and (later) her interest in the substance of his ministry:

> In the midst of my preaching the ague came upon me, so that word was sent to the College ... This comes to the ears of her Ladyship. She inquires into particulars. How long I had been the subject of this – what had been done. The doctor was sent for, and she most kindly inquires into every particular. I

returned on the Monday; was ordered to bed; a prescription was prepared; I was to take it very frequently; one and another was ordered to attend me ...

... The afternoon before we set off, her Ladyship came into the study, and very kindly and spiritually addressed all the students then present. She observed, we dealt with abundance of jewels, but Christ was the Jewel of jewels. He, said she, is the pearl of great price. She gave us most excellent advice how to preach. She prayed for us; then she left us.

Samuel Eyles Pierce, *A True Outline and Sketch of the Life of Samuel Eyles Pierce, written by himself*, London, 1824, pp. 56 & 57.

Lady Huntingdon's response to Pierce's illness was not at all exceptional. Concern for the students' health often appears in the correspondence. Nor was she afraid to be directly involved in their treatment. One of the most touching of all the references to Lady Huntingdon and her students comes in a letter from a young man who wrote simply:

I have not forgot before God my Ladys going on her knee to dress my legs ...

Benjamin Wase to Lady Huntingdon, n.d. E4/3(6A), CF.

Maybe, as some have commented, Lady Huntingdon's relations with her students became a substitute for the close bond she failed to achieve with her own children. Maybe, also, she found it easier to establish such a relationship with social inferiors who were dependent on her – and who did what she told them. Certainly she got very cross with students who disobeyed. But this does not diminish the attractive picture that emerges from her association with the Trevecca students. It goes some way to counterbalance the difficult and authoritarian impression that we get from some other aspects of her life.

At least 212 men passed through Trevecca during its 23 years' existence. We do not know what happened to them all. Some may have gone back to secular jobs. But the majority would have stayed in ministry, whether in the Connexion, other evangelical groups, the Church of England, or Dissenting churches. This meant that Trevecca, despite all its short-comings, had a substantial impact upon the religious life of England in the late eighteenth and early nineteenth centuries. Nor was Trevecca's legacy confined to the individual churches and congregations in which its former students served. The example of Trevecca was an important influence, at the end of the eighteenth century, on the founding of a number of Dissenting colleges, evangelical in theology, and specifically directed (like Trevecca) to fostering ministerial skills. The fact that these later colleges may have been in every way better organized and better taught than Trevecca does not detract from the pioneering work that had begun in Lady Huntingdon's South Wales farmhouse.

15

Secession from the Church of England

꒜꒦

'S: Huntingdon Seceder' was how Lady Huntingdon styled herself in 1787, when she signed the proposed constitution for the new college that was planned as successor to Trevecca. It was a striking way to define herself. It seemed to imply that the most important thing about her was that she had left the Church of England. It was not only in respect of Lady Huntingdon herself that the term appears: for some while the phrase 'the Plan of Secession' was used almost as a way of describing the Connexion itself. Secession was clearly seen as a hugely important step. Despite this, it is surprisingly difficult to say just what secession consisted of, or when it happened. There were broadly two aspects to secession. One concerned the legal position of the Connexion's chapels; the other was the Connexion's ability to ordain its own ministers. Of these, it was the former that precipitated the breach with the Church. The latter, however, was of much greater practical importance, since it affected the week-by-week worship of the Connexion's congregations. We shall start by looking at that aspect.

Lady Huntingdon was born into the Church of England, and for a long while was content to stay there. All her early ministry was conducted within the Church, and most of the prominent evangelical preachers of the day were Anglican clergymen. She probably had no great attachment to the Church as an institution, and she certainly deplored those aspects of it that worked against the spread of evangelical Christianity. But whatever she thought at the start about the long-term nature of her Connexion, she probably assumed that the Church of England would remain what we might call its 'parent body'. In particular she would have expected that her ministers would continue to be Anglican clergy.

Lady Huntingdon's hope, when she founded Trevecca, was thus that her students would be ordained by the Church. There were two reasons why this was important. The first was the long-term problem the students faced if they were not ordained. The rapid spread of the Connexion in the 1770s showed that lay preachers could achieve a great deal without ordination. But they could not sustain congregations on a long-term basis, since (not being ordained) they could not administer Holy Communion. Students themselves would be unhappy at remaining in this anomalous position for too long, so there was a danger that they would be poached away to ministry (and ordination) with Dissenting congregations. This was the second reason why securing Anglican ordination for the students was important.

It proved, however, a near impossible task. We saw earlier, when looking at the students' involvement in overseas mission, that one of the two men who went to Bencoolen in 1770 was successful in obtaining ordination, but that Lady Huntingdon had to give up hopes of ordination for the students going to Bethesda, two years later. Only a handful of other Trevecca men were ordained in the 1770s, and then only after much effort and often rigorous examination. Here, for example, is James Glazebrook describing the examination that accompanied his ordination as a deacon in 1771. The treatment he received was considerate. But the questions were searching and there was clearly deep suspicion, about both the nature of Trevecca College and how far the students were expected to hold extreme Calvinist doctrines:

I have this day past an examination before the Bishop's chaplain. I have reason to conclude (by his method of examining me) that some caution had been given him concerning me ... He gave me the 3rd of St John to read ... [and] then gave me the 11th and 12th Articles to translate [i.e., the Church of England Articles dealing with justification by faith and the status of good works] ... After I had answered his questions on those articles, he put to me the last clause of the 17th article [on how to approach predestination] ... I told him that I could not hold the doctrine of reprobation [predestination to damnation], and yet I was persuaded ... that God did *particularly* call some, and *generally others* ...

When we had done he invited me to have a dish of chocolate and told me he found that I had dipped into many of the deep things of the Gospel, and said that it was so far praiseworthy.

The Bishop ... asked me whether I was not educated at Lady Huntingdon's Academy ... He then asked me who they were who came there ... [and] whether Lady Huntingdon did not oblige the young men to embrace the doctrines of Reprobation and Irresistible Grace ...

He said Mr Chelsom (the chaplain) has cleared up my doubts very well concerning you ... He asked me several other questions, such as whether your Ladyship was at all the expense in providing for all the young men, and what age they were of when they were taken in.

Glazebrook to Lady Huntingdon, 13 & 16 December 1771. F1/152, 153, CF.

This was not the end of Glazebrook's ordination problems: he did not achieve the next stage, ordination to the priesthood, till 1777. Nevertheless, he was lucky to make it at all. More then 200 men were associated with Trevecca College, over its 24-year existence, but barely 20 became Anglican clergymen. To add insult to injury, so far as Lady Huntingdon was concerned, some of these were only successful because they went on for a spell to Oxford or Cambridge, after Trevecca. When Trevecca started, some evangelical ministers thought that none of her students would ever be ordained. Obviously they were wrong. But Lady Huntingdon, who had a natural tendency to suspect that people were conspiring against her, became convinced that there was a concerted policy:

> I have from good authority that the bishops have entered into combination never to ordain any that is brought up by me, nay further, nor any that knows me, or ever had any connection with me. And of these latter, should they ever have any offer, in the presence of three clergy they are publicly to disown all my principles and all knowledge or connection with me hereafter.

Lady Huntingdon to William Piercy, 22 September 1773. A4/3(2B), CF.

It was not only the attitude of the bishops that could cause problems for would-be ordinands. Before he could be ordained, a man had to have notice of his intended ordination read out in church, he had to have signed testimonials, and he had to have the offer of a curacy where he would serve his 'title'. Any of these could run into difficulties with obstructive clergy. Finding curacies posed a particular problem: they depended upon there being a sympathetic incumbent who had a vacancy for a curate at just the right time.

Lady Huntingdon must sometimes have wondered whether it was worth all the trouble – especially as those newly ordained went off to serve their curacies, and would be lost to the Connexion, at least for the moment. Some returned later to give occasional assistance, but none came back full-time. An alternative to Anglican ordination was ordination by Dissenters, and some Trevecca students went down this route. But this too meant losing the man concerned to the congregation to which he had been ordained. Nor was Dissenting ordination all that easy to obtain. Dissenting ministers could be just as suspicious as Anglican bishops of the evangelical theology and low academic standards that they associated with Trevecca. So Dissenting ordination was not a long-term solution, either.

The only other answer was for the Connexion to ordain its own ministers. There is a small, but important, piece of evidence that Lady Huntingdon was considering this from as early as 1775. It comes in a letter from Glascott, after the failure of yet another Trevecca student to secure Anglican ordination:

> I am more and more persuaded of the utility of some kind of ordination for the students, and as the Bishops seem determined to reject them, I often wish the plan your Ladyship had in agitation last winter had been put into execution.

Glascott to Lady Huntingdon, 1 June 1776. F1/1729, CF.

There is another tantalizing reference in 1778, to what was then termed 'itinerant ordination'. As in 1775 and 1776, nothing further appears to have happened. Thus we do not know quite what Lady Huntingdon had in mind. For all her eccentricity and self-belief, we can be pretty certain she never considered performing ordinations herself. So, as she had no bishops, she must have envisaged using existing Anglican or Dissenting ministers on the first occasion – probably (since this is what eventually happened in 1783) employing two ministers to perform the ceremony. After that, the men ordained could ordain others, and the process would become self-perpetuating.

If Lady Huntingdon had gone down this road in the 1770s, would it have implied that she had left the Church of England? When John Wesley introduced Methodist ordinations in the following decade, he claimed that this was not an act of separation. Lady Huntingdon might conceivably have said the same. Her Connexion would still have been served occasionally by Anglican clergy, and she could have argued that her own ministers were simply filling the gaps in between. The Connexion would certainly have been a strange hybrid, so far as Anglican church law was concerned. At some times its congregations would receive 'valid' Holy Communion from an Anglican clergyman; at others the sacrament would come from a Connexion minister whose ordination was not recognized by the Church. That, in fact, is exactly the situation that happened *after* she had seceded: beneficed Anglican clergy continued to give occasional service at the Connexion's chapels, alongside its own ministers.

This debate is of course somewhat academic, since Lady Huntingdon did not start ordinations till after she had left the Church of England. But it is interesting that she should have considered ordinations long before she had thoughts of leaving.

As implied at the start of this chapter, it was a dispute over the legal position of chapels that actually led to the Connexion's secession. To understand this, we need to remind ourselves how the law applied in the eighteenth century. The Toleration Act, passed after the Glorious Revolution of 1688, did not abolish the old penal laws against Dissenters. Instead, it provided exemption from those laws for places of worship and for preachers ('of any congregation of dissenting Protestants') which were duly registered in accordance with the Act's requirements. That was fine so far as the old Dissenting denominations were concerned. It was not so good for evangelicals from the Church of England who did not want to be labelled as Dissenters. John Wesley agonized for a long time over whether the Toleration Act applied to Methodists at all; in his view the Act concerned dissenters from the Established Church, and had no relevance to a group who wanted to remain loyal to the Church. But there were arguments both ways, and practice varied considerably within Wesleyan Methodism in respect of the registration of both preachers and premises.

The issues were similar for the Connexion, but with an important difference. As we have seen, Lady Huntingdon was entitled, as a peeress, to appoint domestic chaplains, and to open private chapels that were exempt from the requirement to register under the Toleration Act. Lady Huntingdon certainly appointed chaplains, but does not seem to have set much store by this particular privilege – probably because the entitlement was limited to two appointments at a time. The right to private chapels was much more significant, and many of her chapels were treated as 'protected' in this way. Sometimes a case could be made out to justify this. In the case of some of the early chapels, like Brighton, Bath and Tunbridge Wells, there was a house attached – so Lady Huntingdon could reasonably claim that the chapel was there for her convenience, when she was in residence. (The former Bath chapel is an excellent surviving example of a chapel and chapel-house complex.) That defence became weaker as chapels grew in number, and were established in places that Lady Huntingdon had never visited. For 20 years, however, the legal fiction went unchallenged. In most instances, Lady Huntingdon would not have worried very much if it had been. Unlike Wesley, she did not seem concerned about her congregations being termed 'Dissenters'. She was content, where circumstances made this appropriate, for them to register their chapels under the Toleration Act. During the 1770s a number did so. There are also many instances of her itinerant preachers being invited to officiate in non-Connexion premises that were licensed under the Toleration Act. No-one suggested that this meant the Connexion had seceded from the Church of England.

It was because of one individual chapel, acquired by Lady Huntingdon in 1779, that secession eventually took place. Despite the rapid spread of her work in the years after Trevecca was founded in 1768, it was a while before Lady Huntingdon had a major chapel of her own in London. From 1773 she was associated with a congregation meeting in temporary premises in Wapping, but no permanent Connexion chapel was built there until 1778. And it did not measure up to her desire for a significant base in the capital. In 1776 she became aware that the lease had become available on a large place of entertainment, built as a rotunda and called The Pantheon. This was off the Farringdon Road in Clerkenwell. Lady Huntingdon considered taking it over and converting it into a chapel, but her friends persuaded her that it was too far from fashionable London for her purposes. She did no more about it at that stage. Others were more optimistic about its potential as a chapel, however. These were two evangelical Anglican clergymen, not linked with Lady Huntingdon, Herbert Jones and William Taylor. This is how Lady Huntingdon was later to describe what happened:

> Originally the place now called Northampton chapel [the name given to the premises by Jones and Taylor] was an elegant building erected at a great expense for public diversions, and soon became so abounding in wicked practices that the civil magistrate was obliged to put it down ... Messrs Taylor and Jones took it and by various and proper alterations made it one of the most beautiful places of worship ... to contain between three and four thousand hearers ... By three different disappointments of its being protected by Peers ... [they were] obliged ... to license it under the Toleration [Act], but continued the regular services of the Church & had gathered by their unwearied labours a very large and serious congregation.
>
> Lady Huntingdon to ?, n.d. E3/2(16), CF.

It was the source of the 'large congregation' that caused the trouble. The parish of St James, Clerkenwell, in which the chapel was situated, was unusual because of the arrangements for paying its vicar, the Revd William Sellon. Sellon received only a tiny stipend, and was dependent for most of his income on contributions from his congregation. This meant that it was a very serious matter when a significant proportion of that congregation transferred to the new chapel. (To give an idea of the implications for Sellon, his total annual income, from St James's and from the other clerical appointments he held, was around £1,300.

But his *assured* stipend and fees from the parish were less than £11.) Early in 1778 Sellon initiated proceedings against Jones and Taylor in the relevant church court (the consistory court of the Bishop of London). The charge against them was that they had, as Anglican clergymen, taken services in premises that were licensed under the Toleration Act. Their crime was one that was far from uncommon, and was often winked at. But judgement, when it was eventually given in February 1779, was against them. They could no longer officiate at the chapel, and services were continued for the moment by Dissenting ministers.

Lady Huntingdon had had plenty of time to decide a plan of action, and took immediate steps to acquire the lease of the chapel. In a letter to the Bishop of London she claimed to be acting out of concern for the interests of the Church:

> In consequence of some precipitate steps taken by the Revd Messrs Taylor and Jones, they have incurred such a censure as I am sorry to say justice has [been] determined against them. From this many and great difficulties attend them. The alternative is either to dissent from the Church, or very unjustly to break through their engagement to a congregation raised by their faithful labours ... My interposition appeared the means to prevent ... some thousands becoming Dissenters ... I have agreed to take [the chapel] and to protect it regularly under the Church.

> Lady Huntingdon to the Bishop of London, 25 February 1779. E3/2(3), CF.

The chapel was closed for a few weeks while other alterations were made. The important symbolic change was the creation of a passage-way between the chapel and the adjoining house (thereafter referred to as 'her Ladyship's House'), into which she now moved. The message was clear: this was Lady Huntingdon's home, and the chapel was her personal place of worship. At the end of March the chapel reopened, under its new name of 'Spa

Fields'. It was no longer registered under the Toleration Act but relied upon her protection as a peeress.

Before the end of April Sellon began proceedings against Thomas Haweis, who had been running Spa Fields since it reopened. Haweis challenged the competence of the consistory court to hear the case, on the grounds that both he and the chapel were protected by rights of peerage, and thus outside the court's jurisdiction. Lady Huntingdon was advised she would win on this point, 'and thus we shall tread upon the serpent . . . and all the powers of darkness'. Her confidence was misplaced. The court ruled against Haweis's claim in June 1779, and then began leisurely consideration of the substantive issues. Before judgement was given, Sellon had initiated a similar action against Glascott, one of the clergy who had now followed Haweis at the chapel. Sellon's case was a simple one: how could a chapel seating thousands, accessed by a public entrance, and for which tickets were sold, possibly count as a private chapel? The court agreed. In May 1780, judgement was given against Haweis, and he was admonished not to preach there again.

Lady Huntingdon had already decided what she should do if the judgement went against her. Leaving the Church was her only option. The following extracts show both the dramatic terms in which she viewed the situation before the judgement, and the pained terms in which some of her key ministers set out the grounds for separation afterwards:

I at present see that unless they allow me my rights I will secede, being resolved that Christ shall be magnified in life and death and the loss of all things . . . If they are permitted to turn us out, woe, woe be to them. Death and hell will follow fast upon their heels . . . For more than forty years we have suffered contempt for our confession of the Son of God & he has delivered, & I trust will yet deliver us, from this bondage.

Lady Huntingdon to Mrs Wills, 3 September 1779. JRL ENG. MSS 338.

By a late decision in the Consistory court of the Bishop of London it appears that her Ladyship cannot authorise us to officiate in her chapels in the public manner wherein we have been accustomed to exercise our ministry . . . We think there is no alternative left, but for us to secede or withdraw peaceably from the established Church; & under the protection of the Toleration Act continue to maintain her doctrines, though we cannot in all things submit to her discipline.

The Revds Glascott, Wills and Taylor to the Archbishops and Bishops of the Church of England, 30 June 1780. E3/3(11), CF.

The letter to the bishops was clearly carefully prepared, like the several drafts that exist of a letter for Lady Huntingdon herself to send to the Archbishop. Yet neither item was sent. The fact was that Lady Huntingdon was now faced with sustained resistance to secession among some of her key ministers. This should have come as no surprise. Haweis, for example, was strongly loyal to the Church of England, and had been arguing for several years that the Connexion needed a visible Anglican centre. This implied having three or four major chapels, which would be protected by Lady Huntingdon's rights as a peeress, and be served only by clergymen. This inner core would be distinct from the rest of the Connexion's work, which could operate under the Toleration Act as necessary. This arrangement would prevent the Connexion being over-influenced by Dissent.

Once it was mooted that the Connexion as a whole should secede from the Church, other voices were raised in objection. Two of Lady Huntingdon's other clergy associates, Henry Peckwell and Thomas Pentycross, argued that the legal judgement on Spa Fields need not affect other parts of the Connexion. Those other chapels that were currently covered by Lady Huntingdon's protection – which had not been challenged anywhere else – should continue as before. Some prominent lay members of the Connexion were also opposed. And when Lady Huntingdon sought support from the Welsh evangelical clergy, she received a cautious response. One of them said of a colleague: 'I would as soon hope to persuade the Pope to become Lutheran, as prevail with him to coincide with the late proposal.'

Lady Huntingdon remained convinced of the need for a general secession, but took no immediate steps in this direction. Haweis had appealed against the earlier judgement, and that appeal was still theoretically under consideration until the case petered out in the spring of the following year, 1781. The spotlight was now on Glascott, especially when it became clear in April that Sellon was determined to pursue the case against him. The Spa Fields committee, with an anxious eye on the finances of the chapel, argued for immediate secession. Lady Huntingdon identified the clergy that she thought should take the lead in leaving the Church, but now favoured a low-key approach:

> Mr Glascott's secession appears absolutely necessary ... In consultation with two of the most judicious friends it appeared clearly to us all that Mr Glascott should without delay set out privately for Cambridge & return directly to Spa Fields & continue to go on just as he now does, only omitting some prayer (as that for the Bishop etc.). Mr Wills to succeed him & as soon as cited take the same method ... without any public noise of any kind or notice to the people whatever ... I would readily give my attendance, but should this manner of acting meet with general approbation, the less this could be considered proper.
>
> ... should any distress follow to any of you on my account, this I could so ill bear ... To prison I am ready to go with you all.
>
> Lady Huntingdon to the committee of Spa Fields chapel, 22 April 1781, and to Cradock Glascott, 8 June 1781. E4/10(10) & (11), CF.

The image of Lady Huntingdon in an eighteenth-century prison would have made a striking subject for William Hogarth (had he still been alive), but her resolve on this point was not tested. Nor was Glascott's, whose 'apostolic spirit' led him in a different path from the one she had envisaged. He delayed any immediate action on secession, and then in the autumn informed her that he had agreed to be vicar of a parish in Devon. She was not best pleased. With bitter irony, she told him she bore no resentment, only grief – and then added: 'Never, never, never forget that in the height of God's greatest honours upon you, you have the misery of knowing you have declined his services.'

Glascott's departure from the scene meant that when the consistory court finally found against him in December 1781, he was not personally affected. The court's decision showed, however, that Lady Huntingdon had no hope of going on as before. The result was the secession of Thomas Wills, who had been serving full-time in the Connexion since 1778. Once the decision was taken, events moved quickly, as shown by entries in the Spa Fields Minute Book:

7th January [1782]. Special Meeting addressed by Mr Wills ... Mr Wills declared his willingness to secede & his grounds for secession, being really a Dissenter from principle, ... there being several particulars [in the Church service] in his judgement very objectionable – for instance, in the baptismal office, where the minister gives God thanks that the baptised child is regenerated etc. and in the burial service where he is obliged to express a sure and certain hope of a joyful Resurrection, be the character of the deceased what it may. Mr Wills said further he could not consent to be under canonical jurisdiction ...

11th and 12th January. All the Committee ... signed a requisition to the Bishop of London to register the chapel a dissenting meeting-house: and Mr Wills having qualified himself [as a Dissenter] at the Quarter Sessions at Hicks Hall on Saturday the 12th, signed the same and the chapel was accordingly licensed the same day.

Spa Fields Minute Book. D1/1, pp. 17–18, CF.

It was an important step, but it fell far short of a 'general secession' by the Connexion. It meant that Wills could officiate lawfully at Spa Fields, but that any other clergyman could still be challenged unless he himself had seceded. So the search was on for more secessions. The ideal would have been to have a number of ex-Anglican clergy, but Lady Huntingdon needed at least one more. This was because she had returned to the idea of a Connexion ordination, and wanted two ministers to perform the ceremony. After the earlier resistance shown to secession, and then Glascott's refusal, Lady Huntingdon must have realized that this was going to be difficult. So it proved. In April 1782 she lamented that she did not know of a single minister who would secede. (Characteristically, this was because 'all seem seeking too much their own, but not the things of Jesus Christ'.) Eventually she persuaded William Taylor, one of the original founders of the Northampton Chapel. Many months were spent negotiating the terms under which he would serve if he seceded, but eventually he took the step in January 1783, a full year after Wills.

The way was now clear for the Connexion to start ordaining its own ministers. In preparation for this, Articles of Faith had been drawn up for the Connexion. Many of these were quoted verbatim from the Church of England's own Thirty-Nine Articles. This was done deliberately, in order to show that the Connexion was not departing from the fundamental beliefs of the Church. One of the main additions to the Church Articles was a reference to a key Calvinist doctrine: the belief that the righteousness of Christ is imputed to sinners. Interestingly, however, the Connexion also added words clearly meant to guard against antinomianism, by emphasizing the importance of believers practising holiness in their lives.

The ordination itself took place at Spa Fields on 9 March 1783. Six students were ordained, with Wills and Taylor as the officiating ministers. Curiously, Lady Huntingdon herself was not present, though this may simply have been on health grounds: the main part of the service went on for five hours, and was then followed by a Communion. The ordination was a radical step, and it caused controversy inside the Connexion, as well as outside. An account of the service was later published, in order, it was said, to vindicate the actions of those who took part 'to the Christian world in general, as well as for the information and satisfaction of the various congregations in our connexion'. During the service Wills had spent some time responding to criticisms from Dissenters that he had no authority for what he was doing:

> ... if we trace up the dissenting church to its first rise, shall we not find their ministers, of that time, were episcopally ordained? ... Were they not afterwards reduced to the necessity of ordaining among themselves? What right had *they* thus to ordain, that *we* had not in *similar circumstances*? ...
>
> An Authentic Narrative of the Primary Ordination, London, 1784.

Other ordination services followed quickly after the first, so that within four years some 30 to 40 new ministers had been added to the Connexion's ranks.

The printed account of the ordination included the secession statement that had been prepared back in 1780. There is no evidence that any direct use was ever made of the latter. Maybe publishing it in this way was seen as the formal announcement of the Connexion's departure from the Church of England. This was quite important, because it is otherwise difficult to say quite how things had altered as a result of secession. Only Spa Fields was affected: the chapel was now lawful (and untouchable) while served by clergy who had seceded, or by the Connexion's own ministers. Nothing had to change at any other chapel, unless the local incumbent challenged it in the way that Sellon had done at Spa Fields.

The rest of the Connexion seems to have gone on much as before. Not all chapels were immediately licensed: for example, Bath continued unlicensed until 1788. And clergy who had not left the Church of England could still preach for the Connexion. One example of this was Glascott, who was restored to Lady Huntingdon's favour very quickly. As early as 1783 he offered to spend periods of time away from his Devon parish in order to preach in the Connexion. He continued serving in this way through into the next century. He was not the only clergyman to combine parish duties with occasional service in the post-secession Connexion. It is true that some prominent evangelical clergy who had worked with Lady Huntingdon in the early days of the Connexion – men like Romaine, Berridge and Venn – are absent from its records in this later period. They may well have disapproved of Lady Huntingdon's decision to secede. Romaine certainly did. But most had ceased to be actively involved before the events we have been describing.

One effect of secession was to create the odd situation in which Anglican and ex-Anglican clergy worked alongside one another in the Connexion. This was to lead to tension, as we shall see in the final chapter.

16

Lady Huntingdon's Last Years

❦

By the time of the Connexion's first ordinations, Lady Huntingdon was 75 years old. She had another eight years of life before her, and those years were to be as active as any that had gone before. This was partly the result of the ordinations themselves. They meant that the Connexion had become self-supporting, and was no longer dependent on outside help to maintain the sacramental life of its congregations. So the Connexion shed its provisional character, and had arrived as a permanent part of the religious scene.

That scene had become increasingly complex by the later eighteenth century. The evangelical world had become a market place, with many different groups competing for ministers and adherents. This fact, together with the Connexion's own growth, made the task for Lady Huntingdon more difficult. There were more chapels to be supplied with ministers; more issues over chapel-building schemes and leases; and more outside congregations seeking to join the Connexion. Those were the upsides of success, but there were downsides as well. The Connexion had become a source of ordained manpower, so there was an increased danger that its ministers would be poached by other congregations. The expectations placed on Lady Huntingdon's limited financial resources became greater than ever. And the more complex an organization the Connexion became, the more chances there were of mistakes being made. Where this happened, leaving congregations with inadequate ministers or with no minister at all, congregations were quite likely to look elsewhere for help – as the following example shows:

[We] return your Ladyship thanks for so many valuable supplies we have been favoured with under your Ladyship's patronage ... It is with grief that I inform you that some of the last supplies sent by your Ladyship, and the various disappointments experienced made us determine ... to solicit the assistance of Dr Addington [a Dissenting minister, and former pupil of Doddridge, who ran an academy in London]. Therefore ... we must beg leave to decline troubling your Ladyship any further ... it being our intention to have a settled pastor.

Edward Hill (on behalf of the Berkhamstead congregation) to Lady Huntingdon, 2 March 1788. F1/712, CF.

Berkhamstead's reference to a settled pastor is symbolic of the growing resistance that Lady Huntingdon encountered to her cherished system of moving itinerant preachers in rapid rotation around her congregations. It is not difficult to see why she wanted to preserve the practice: it gave her much greater influence and control over congregations than if ministers settled with them for indefinite periods. As we have seen, however, there were good reasons why many ministers and congregations disliked it. However exciting itinerancy might seem at the start, most ministers would eventually tire of it: it meant continually having to get to know new congregations, it generally involved having to live in lodgings, and it implied never being able to put down roots or to start a family. Congregations too favoured continuity, and the opportunity to develop a relationship with their minister. And once they had found someone they liked, they would want to keep him – rather than take a chance on who they might get next.

Lady Huntingdon did not have to run the Connexion entirely on her own. A major helper was Lady Anne Erskine (1739–1804), daughter of a Scottish earl, who had been her friend since the 1760s. Lady Anne became increasingly involved in the organization of the Connexion during Lady Huntingdon's final years. By the end, as we shall see, her influence was decisive. From 1784 Lady Huntingdon also had professional help, in the person of a secretary, George Best. Best's role was not that of a scribe: Lady Huntingdon continued to write her own letters, right to the end. Rather, he took over some of the administrative tasks that would otherwise have fallen to her, and he advised her how to handle others – for example, highlighting the questions to be addressed before she signed a chapel deed. Best's assistance did not mean that Lady Huntingdon ceased to be involved in day-to-day matters: even on her death-bed she was still taking a close interest in the deployment of ministers. But Best did help to make the burden of business more bearable, and he occasionally took trips on her behalf. This included Trevecca, which Lady Huntingdon did not visit after 1787.

Lady Huntingdon's failure to return to the college, during the final years of her life, is in marked contrast to the extended periods she had spent there earlier. Her visits had sometimes amounted to many months on end, including one stay of nearly two years in the mid 1780s. Did her absence imply that Lady Huntingdon had lost interest in the college? It would be strange if it did, because the introduction of the Connexion's own ordination had made it even more important than before to have a regular supply of young men with some form of ministerial training. Moreover, Lady Huntingdon had previously set great store on having personal contact with the students, and influencing the development of their individual vocations. Although the college's days at Trevecca were drawing to an end, because of the imminent expiration of the lease, Lady Huntingdon was actively exploring new locations – one criterion for which, so she implied in 1790, was that it should be easier for her to reach. She was also, as we shall see in a moment, considering what needed to be done to continue the college after her death. It was certainly not indifference to the institution that kept her away during her last years. Perhaps it was simply that London had become the administrative hub of the Connexion, and it was convenient to stay put, unless there were pressing reasons to be elsewhere. In any case, there were other schemes demanding her attention.

One of the striking things about Lady Huntingdon (whether or not this was always a good thing) was her boundless interest in new enterprises, including ones that implied her travelling long distances at an advanced age. We saw before how she toyed with the idea of moving to America in 1783. Over the following years her interest in overseas mission widened to embrace continental Europe. The conversion of Roman Catholics seems to have been as important to her as the conversion of native Americans, and in 1787 she was thrilled to learn of an apparent opening for the Connexion in Brussels. She was told that there were over 600 Protestant families in the city – by implication, all eager for the Connexion's ministrations – and she secured a large chapel there for the use of her ministers. More than that, she decided to go to Brussels in person. Thomas Wills was to accompany her, and expectations were high: one correspondent even suggested that she extend her travel plans to include Ostend, where he had heard there was another Protestant church in need of a minister. But everything then began to unravel. First Lady Huntingdon and Wills missed the ship they were due to take to the continent. This was reminiscent of the Trevecca students trying to get to Bethesda, 14 years earlier, and it proved an equally bad omen. Reports arrived to the effect that the whole venture had been a popish plot designed to lure Lady Huntingdon abroad and assassinate her. The alleged instigator of this scheme was a Lord Douglass, who purported to be a convert from Catholicism, and who was the person who first interested Lady Huntingdon in the Brussels venture. The sudden death of Lord Douglass, on the eve of Lady Huntingdon's planned departure, was seen as a clear sign of divine retribution. Whether or not there really had been a plot – or just an elaborate hoax – Wills used the events to dissuade Lady Huntingdon from pursuing the venture further. He had evidently not been much attracted to it in the first place:

No pen nor tongue can describe the overflowing of my poor grateful heart . . . for . . . deliverance of us all out of the hands of our popish & hellish adversaries . . . For my own part I can truly say . . . my constant language was 'I have no light from the Lord on this matter; if her Ladyship sees it right to go, I see my duty to attend her . . . I think the Lord will not let us go unless he has work to do by us that I know nothing about'.

. . .though you might not have been devoted to destruction by *gunpowder*, *poison* would have as effectively removed you out of the way. And who knows but the popish massacres would have been acted over again? . . . I expect there will be . . . more baits thrown out . . . pressing your dear Ladyship still to go. But as you have had no call from the Lord yourself . . . I would not have your dear Ladyship attempt it for the whole world . . . I suspect the information of the hundreds of Protestants longing for your coming. But as so few of these understand English, and it is evident the Lord has not given you a special call, how can we expect a blessing?

Wills to Lady Huntingdon, 27 & 30 April 1787. F1/622 & 624, CF.

Lady Huntingdon liked to feel wanted, so Wills's scepticism about her European calling may have contributed to the friction that was to develop between them. But though Lady Huntingdon did not get to Brussels, she remained interested in the continent. Two years later there was still speculation about the possible opening at Ostend. And when the French Revolution broke out, it seemed a God-given opportunity to advance the Protestant cause. With touching naïveté she viewed the Revolution as being principally an attack on Roman Catholicism. She did not see it as an assault on everything that she herself represented and believed in. So in 1790 she devised a scheme to secure a presence for the Connexion in Paris:

> My present plan is to . . . apply . . . to Necker [the French finance minister] and agree for the finest church in Paris. Their finances are *so low* that they will rejoice to have me purchase it.

> France will be for the English protestants if I succeed.

> Lady Huntingdon to Thomas Haweis, 24 March & 13 April 1790. Bridwell Library MS 118, 122.

This time the language issue was not ignored, for she even planned to include French and Flemish on the college curriculum. Nothing came of these great schemes – although it is not clear quite when it dawned upon Lady Huntingdon that revolutionary France was not the best place for the followers of an evangelical countess.

Despite these exotic distractions, there were more practical matters demanding Lady Huntingdon's attention. A major issue, as implied above, was what to do about the college. Its future location was one problem. From the mid 1780s various alternative sites were considered, though nothing came of any of them. Of equal concern was how to pay to finance the college in the longer term. Lady Huntingdon had largely funded Trevecca from her own resources, and latterly (as demands on those resources increased) the college struggled hard to make ends meet. In the last years the housekeeper faced continual headaches in paying bills and fending off creditors. Clearly matters could not go on like this. So in 1787 a meeting was called in London, involving Lady Huntingdon and a group of prominent London ministers and laymen. The outcome was the establishment of a society intended to perpetuate an institution on the lines of Trevecca.

Such a college would be meant principally (though not exclusively) for men intending to serve in the Connexion. The evangelistic purpose of the enterprise was emphasized by the name they chose: the Apostolic Society.

Whether the initiative for the initial meeting came from Lady Huntingdon or from the laity at Spa Fields is not clear: the manuscripts give conflicting information on the point. Either way, the creation of the Apostolic Society shows how power was beginning to pass from Lady Huntingdon's hands. It is interesting that the future trustees of the Society declined to begin fund-raising until they had received clear ground rules for the new college. It is even more striking that the response they received (probably drafted by George Best) addressed many of the criticisms that had been made about Trevecca. For example, a regular complaint had been that Trevecca students were sent out too quickly, to the detriment of their studies, and before they were properly prepared for ministry. So the proposed rules of the new college specified the length and contents of the course that students were to receive, and the minimum time they were to spend in college before being sent out to preach. It was a tacit admission of where things had gone wrong at Trevecca. But if Lady Huntingdon was prepared to contemplate what should happen in the future, she was not willing to concede authority immediately. While she lived, the only role for the Apostolic Society was to raise funds for the future college (not for Trevecca), and this may well account for the comparatively meagre amounts that were subscribed in the first years.

One person who was unhappy about the creation of the Apostolic Society was Thomas Wills. This was not because he thought all was well with Trevecca – indeed, possibly the reverse. Back in 1783 he had expressed doubts whether residential training was necessarily a good or effective use of resources. One of the alternative suggestions he made was to leave ministerial candidates in their secular jobs, while they studied part-time under an experienced minister. He had lost that argument. But if there *were* to be a college, he did not think that lay people should have a role in its direction, as implied by the plans for the Apostolic Society. His negative views on the Society, combined with his scepticism over Lady Huntingdon's European ventures, contributed to the breach that occurred between them in 1788.

At this distance of time, the split appears wholly unnecessary, and one that Lady Huntingdon should have taken all possible steps to avoid. Wills was related to her by marriage, and they had been personally very close; he had given up his Church of England appointment to serve her; he had seceded from the Church (so there was no chance of him going back to a parish); and he had an effective and popular ministry in the Connexion. All was not well, however, between Wills and two other ex-clergymen colleagues, William Taylor and John Bradford. Bradford had joined the Connexion soon after the secession, but there were theological differences between him and Wills. Bradford held strong Calvinist views, and taught that because the believer was saved by God's grace, he was not bound by the moral law; Wills feared this would lead to immorality, and he argued the need for Christians to grow in holiness. Their differences led to opposing factions forming within the Spa Fields congregation. At this stage, in 1787–88, it was Bradford who stood higher in Lady Huntingdon's regard, despite some pretty immature behaviour on his part (on one occasion he even dressed himself up to look like Wills). Wills made the mistake of writing to Taylor about the situation, possibly in terms that implied doubts about Lady Huntingdon's judgement. Taylor saw an opportunity to score over the man who was his rival as the leading minister of the Connexion, and he showed the letters to Lady Huntingdon. It was the beginning of the end, and within a few months Wills had been summarily dismissed from the Connexion. Lady Huntingdon was bitter, especially at what she viewed as an insinuation that she was becoming senile:

... on my dismissing of Mr Wills two accusations lie against me by him: one as in error and antinomianism, & the other as if my intellect was gone. This after ten years the most tender of him and his wife in every instance ... [it is] the greatest cruelty flesh and blood could well sustain.

Lady Huntingdon to Nathaniel Rowlands, 25 July 1788. NLW deposit 350A.

Lady Huntingdon refused Wills's request to preach a farewell sermon at Spa Fields, so he published one instead. This ended with an implicit reminder to Lady Huntingdon of the support he enjoyed within the congregation: he suggested that it was for the best that he had not been allowed to preach, as *their* tears at his departure would have broken him. Wills had some justification for thinking he would be missed. A number of other Connexion ministers resigned in protest at his dismissal, and a fall-off in support at both the Bath and Bristol chapels was attributed to the same cause.

If Wills's rivals felt any triumph at his fall, however, it was short-lived. Both Taylor and Bradford were dismissed within the following two years: Taylor on a (substantiated) charge of adultery, and Bradford because his antinomianism was proving divisive within the Connexion. In the case of the latter, there was no sharp break, as with Wills. After several months of mounting hostility from Lady Huntingdon, Bradford was left to 'assume' that he had been dismissed. This was perhaps a sign that in the last year of her life Lady Huntingdon's iron will was losing its focus. But one thing was constant: each fall from grace occasioned amendments to Lady Huntingdon's will, so that by her death Wills, Taylor and Bradford were all proscribed from ever preaching again in the Connexion.

Even without the loss of these key ministers, it had been apparent for some time that plans should be made for the organization of the Connexion after Lady Huntingdon's death. This was not

a new concern: ideas for carrying on the work had been discussed since the 1760s. The trouble was that there were several
conflicting interest groups that had to be reconciled in any new
arrangements. One such group were those who fancied themselves in the role of Lady Huntingdon's successor. Running the
Countess of Huntingdon's Connexion might offer little material
reward, but it did promise a great deal of kudos and satisfaction.
There was no-one in her family remotely interested in taking
over, so the hereditary principle did not arise. But Lady Anne
Erskine had had plenty of opportunity to understudy the role,
and clearly saw herself as a natural successor. In the event, as
we shall see, she largely got her way. Then there were ministers
who seem to have had eyes on the top job. Thomas Wills was
one who had some grounds for thinking himself a strong candidate – though in the end, as noted, he chanced his arm too far,
questioned Lady Huntingdon's decisions too many times, and
alienated other ministers who thought that they too had a claim
to run the Connexion. Their triumph over him, as we saw, was
short-lived. They all joined the substantial list of ministers who
might once have been thought leadership candidates, but who
were out of the running before the leader's job fell vacant.

Why did Lady Huntingdon not designate a successor, as Wesley
did at one stage? One reason may have been fear that, if she did
so, she would effectively cede power to that person before she was
ready to hand over. Another factor may have been recognition
of the several competing interest groups that existed within the
Connexion – each of which would have resented domination by
any of the others. For example, chapel committees (on whom,
after all, much of the work of running congregations depended)
were likely to be hostile to arrangements that gave ministers too
much control over them. Conversely, ministers resented lay people having too much authority. They feared the situation in some
Dissenting churches where ministers appeared to be under the
thumb of lay deacons. Even within the ministerial ranks there

were different camps: ministers who had been ordained by the Connexion, clergy who had seceded from the Church of England, and clergy who were still part of the Church. The first two of these groups were likely to resist any arrangements that subordinated them to the third. This was the reason why Wills had opposed plans that Lady Huntingdon formed in 1786 for a trust to run the Connexion:

> You are pleased to mention your new design of appointing a trust of six for the management of the whole Connexion. In the first place I have never been willing it should not always continue immediately under your own direction as long as it pleases God to spare your Ladyship to the Church below. But supposing it is for your own ease & comfort, my dear Madam, to place it in other hands ... I must ... beg leave to submit to you how four clergymen of the Church of England (however respectable they are in themselves) that are neither seceders, nor partial to the secession, are fit to superintend & direct ministers, committees and congregations who are altogether upon that plan.

Wills to Lady Huntingdon, 12 October 1786. F1/1941, CF.

In other words, it was unfair that men who still had the security of a career in the Church of England should have authority over those who had taken the gamble of leaving the Church for the Connexion. Ironically, it was an arrangement on broadly those lines that took over the Connexion after Lady Huntingdon's death.

Before then there had been other suggestions for a collegiate structure to run the Connexion. The most significant was the so-called Plan of Association, drafted by a committee of London ministers and laymen, which was published in 1790, a little over a year before Lady Huntingdon's death. The previous autumn Lady Huntingdon's doctor had advised her to give up running the Connexion altogether, so there was now added urgency to the exercise. The plan is particularly interesting to us in that it contains the fullest surviving list during Lady Huntingdon's lifetime of the congregations that made up her Connexion. Sixty-four places are named, although the list appears incomplete: we know of a few others being served by the Connexion at that time which are not included. The list shows how widely the Connexion had covered the country. In southern England there were chapels from Cornwall in the south-west, across to Kent and East Anglia in the east; there were four London chapels; there was a large concentration in the Midlands, plus a few in Wales; and there were chapels in the north, extending up to Morpeth in the north-east. These congregations were to be grouped into 23 districts, each directed by committees made up of ministers and representative lay people. The whole Connexion would be under a central committee consisting of the London committee, representative laity and ministers from each district, and the trustees of the college.

Lady Huntingdon's excitement over the Plan reveals how concerned she had been about the future:

The long wished for time seems coming by the Plan of an Association of ministers & warm-hearted men over the Connexion to unite for the carrying the Gospel forward ... [so] that when the Lord calls me, my absence will not make more than an old shoe cast aside.

Lady Huntingdon to Thomas Haweis, 25 February 1790. Bridwell Library MS 115.

She hoped somehow to merge her work with that of the Welsh evangelical clergy, and she was thrilled at the thought of the major denomination this would create: 'no yet known Connexion will be so important'.

Alas, it was not to be. The proposals had been structured in such a way that there would always be a lay majority, both

centrally and at district level. This was a bold step for an organization that had previously been run autocratically. And it was
this element of democratic control that most concerned Lady
Anne Erskine (for whom there would have been no future role
in the Connexion) and Thomas Haweis, who had returned to
Lady Huntingdon's service in 1789. Following the departure of
men like Wills and Taylor, Haweis became the most significant
minister in the Connexion. He was forthright in his opposition to the lay and London dominance implicit in the Plan of
Association:

> It is impossible that one person can give another more
> unequivocal evidence of my great desire to serve you . . . And
> at our decease we have destined & left to the service of
> your Ladyship's mission in this place, the chief part of our
> fortune . . . Judge then, my dear Madam, how greatly I am
> astonished, on reading the printed paper, to find that all your
> Ladyship's affairs, & this place [Bath] among the rest, is to
> be delivered up to a society of two-thirds laymen in London,
> & consequently that every minister & his labours are made
> wholly dependent upon them in England . . .
>
>   . . . I very earnestly entreat your Ladyship to consult every
> friend you have . . . and consider if this step proposed will
> not infallibly renew all the divisions . . . which are yet scarcely
> healed . . . If [you are fixed on the Plan], your Ladyship will
> love me, bless me, and dismiss me . . .
>
>   . . . Lady Anne I am sure is your bosom friend & worthy a
> suffrage in this matter.

Haweis to Lady Huntingdon, 12 June 1790. C12/7 & F1/2134, CF.

The views of the congregations had been sought through the
printed circular, mentioned by Haweis, but the response was surprisingly lukewarm. Lady Huntingdon was used to getting her
own way, but this time she accepted defeat. Perhaps she no longer

had the strength or spirit for a fight. In any case she could not afford to alienate Haweis or Lady Anne. So the Plan of Association was dropped, and nothing had been put in its place by the time she died on 17 June 1791.

Lady Huntingdon maintained her interest in the Connexion's affairs right to the last. On the day she died she was concerned to know whether the Welsh clergyman Thomas Charles had agreed to supply at Spa Fields. Her last words were reportedly, 'To know if he comes – that's the point.' Following her death rumours circulated to the effect that her faith had wavered at the end. So Haweis published an account of her passing that included a letter from her doctor, written immediately after the event:

> Let us be thankful that she was preserved to advanced age with the perfect exercise of her mental faculties, and that under long and painful days and nights of sickness, she never repined, but appeared constantly animated in prayer and thankfulness for the unutterable mercies she received . . . A little before she died, she repeatedly said, in a feeble voice just to be heard, 'I shall go to my Father this night'.

> Letter of Dr Lettsom, 18 June 1791, printed in *A Short Account of the Last Days of the Rt Hon. & most respected Lady, Selina, Countess Dowager of Huntingdon* by Thomas Haweis, London, 1791.

Lady Huntingdon's will left her houses, plus the seven chapels that were her personal property, jointly to four beneficiaries: Lady Anne, Haweis and his wife, and her old friend John Lloyd. It seems that the Haweises at least were unaware of the responsibility thus being placed in their hands. In drafting her will Lady Huntingdon had assumed that the Plan of Association would have come into effect as the means for organizing the preachers and dealing with all the other common issues that might arise. In its absence, the beneficiaries found themselves, by default, in the role of trustees running the Connexion. So it was that the

Connexion passed into the control of a non-seceding clergyman and a group of lay people. It would have been Wills's worst nightmare, and he probably thought himself well out of it.

Lady Anne took on the day-to-day affairs of the Connexion and, judging from many of the letters she received from preachers and congregations, things went on much as before. It was to be 30 years after Lady Huntingdon's death, and after the death of the last survivor of the trustees, Thomas Haweis, that a conference was established to guide the affairs of the Connexion. This prolonged autocratic control probably inhibited gifted lay people and ministers in the Connexion from developing their talents as well as they might. This was not in the Connexion's best interests as it sought to establish its place on the nineteenth-century nonconformist scene.

In respect of the college, matters worked out more as Lady Huntingdon had anticipated. The trustees of the Apostolic Society came into their own on her death. They decided that the college should be moved into the London area, and by the autumn of 1791 had found a suitable house at Cheshunt in Hertfordshire. The move out of Trevecca took place in the spring of the following year. After a protracted search, involving discussions with many leading Anglican evangelicals, a serving Church of England clergyman was found to head the new college. Interestingly there was no automatic entry to Cheshunt for the current Trevecca students, who were re-examined prior to admission. This was a sign that Cheshunt, though the successor to Trevecca, was a new and distinctive departure. Nevertheless, the date chosen for the opening of the new college was 24 August – Lady Huntingdon's birthday and the anniversary of the opening of Trevecca. It was a touching acknowledgement of the person whose vision had made it possible.

Had it all been worth it? To pose that question is not the same as asking whether the beliefs that Lady Huntingdon embraced were true, or whether it was right to try to spread them. Such issues are beyond the scope of this book. What we can ask, however, is whether, *taking those beliefs as a given*, Lady Huntingdon used her position and her resources in the way best calculated to promote them.

There is no denying that she achieved a lot, even though her movement was perhaps only a tenth the size of Wesley's. By the time of her death there were over 60 congregations bearing her name, spread right across England and into Wales. There were several thousand people actively involved in congregational life as members of chapel societies, as well as many more who simply attended services. Over 200 men had passed through her training college, which was itself a trail-blazing institution. The college continued as an independent entity – first at Cheshunt in Hertfordshire, and then as Cheshunt College, Cambridge – into the second half of the twentieth century. (The Cheshunt Foundation still exists.) Some 30 to 40 men had been ordained into her Connexion – in the process subscribing to a set of doctrinal articles drawn up specifically for the Connexion's use.

There was nothing unusual in the eighteenth century about starting a new religious denomination – although of course not everyone did it! But to do so as a lay person, *and as a woman*, was pretty striking. We cannot truthfully say that Lady Huntingdon was unique, because she had a Scottish counterpart in Lady Glenorchy. But Lady Glenorchy's sect was tiny in comparison. There was simply nothing comparable to what Lady Huntingdon had achieved.

Nevertheless, the question remains whether the creation of the Connexion represented the best use of the efforts and resources that Lady Huntingdon invested in it.

The Connexion certainly made a difference in the places where it was active. There were many towns and villages that would (for better or for worse) have missed experiencing evangelical religion but for the Connexion's preachers. Despite their estrangement,

Thomas Wills paid this tribute to Lady Huntingdon after her death:

> Thousands, I may say tens of thousands, in various parts of the Kingdom, have heard the gospel through her instrumentality, that in all probability would never have heard it at all.

Memoirs of the Life of the Revd Thomas Wills, by a Friend, 1804, pp. 231–2.

He was surely right in this, especially when one takes into account the many Dissenting congregations that were served by ex-members of the Connexion, or were influenced by its methods and example. It was also the case that Lady Huntingdon's efforts ensured that her particular brand of Calvinistic evangelicalism played a more significant part in the Revival than would otherwise have been the case. There were plenty of Calvinist evangelicals apart from Lady Huntingdon's Connexion, especially in the Church of England and among the followers of George Whitefield. But Lady Huntingdon's followers were an important part of the whole picture. Of course, in terms both of the preaching of her gospel, and of her contribution to Calvinistic Methodism, Lady Huntingdon's legacy might have been stronger had she been able to leave her Connexion with a properly developed structure for its future organization. In the nineteenth century the Connexion grew at a far slower rate than other branches of Methodism. The religious census of 1851 showed that the Connexion had 109 chapels. But this compares with over 6,500 Wesleyan chapels, and more than 4,000 belonging to other Methodist groups.

Even apart from that last point, could she have done more? Some commentators, both in the nineteenth century and in our own time, have suggested an important further achievement: the evangelization of the upper classes. According to this view, Lady Huntingdon made evangelicalism respectable and acceptable among those who shaped and influenced eighteenth-century society – thus paving the way for the return to serious moral and religious values that marked pre-Victorian and Victorian England. That would indeed have been a significant achievement.

It is doubtful, however, how much, if at all, she contributed to this process. It is certainly true that perceptions of the aristocracy changed as the eighteenth century went on. In the second half of the century people increasingly came to believe that the nobility should lead a moral life and set a good example. Expectations grew that peers would involve themselves in public and philanthropic causes. And at the end of the century the horrors of the French Revolution underlined the need for a disciplined and respected ruling class. Lady Huntingdon can hardly be said to have caused these changes, although she was certainly an early example of eighteenth-century moral seriousness. Indeed, many of the peers who patronized philanthropic causes in the later eighteenth century were the husbands or relatives of titled women who had been part of her circle earlier on. In that respect she may certainly have had an influence. But supporting good causes and embracing evangelical beliefs are not the same thing. And it is possible that Lady Huntingdon's authoritarianism and eccentricity did as much to alienate potential aristocratic believers, as attract them. The likelihood was that the more she went on, the more she was seen as a figure of fun, or worse. Extreme religious zeal often does more harm than good, especially when it takes itself too seriously – and there is no evidence that Lady Huntingdon managed to laugh at herself very often. The following comment may well be typical of how some people saw her during her middle years:

> I believe and hope she means well, but she makes herself ridiculous to the profane and dangerous to the good ...

> Mrs Montague in 1756, quoted in Muriel Jaeger, *Before Victoria*, 1956.

Once Lady Huntingdon was managing a popular religious movement – which is essentially what her Connexion had become by the 1770s – she was even further out on a limb. She had made herself an oddity. And though that doubtless made many people *notice* Methodism, perhaps even respect it, that is very different from winning them over.

There are so many 'if only's in the case of Lady Huntingdon. If only she had been gentler and more winsome in dealing with her peers . . .; if only she had persevered in the charitable works that marked her early life, but which were later replaced by evangelism . . .; if only she had not taken sides within the Revival, but had done more to build bridges between the various factions . . . etc., then her legacy might have been very different. She might not have left behind a Countess of Huntingdon's Connexion, and we might not now have been reading about her. But the mark she left upon the hearts and lives of her contemporaries might conceivably have been greater and more beneficial.

Bibliographical Note

There are several important modern works on the eighteenth-century religious scene, especially Alan D. Gilbert, *Religion and Society in Industrial England: Church, Chapel and Social Change, 1740–1914* (London and New York: Longman, 1976); Peter Virgin, *The Church in an Age of Negligence* (Cambridge: James Clarke & Co., 1989); and *The Church of England, c. 1689–c. 1833: From Toleration to Tractarianism*, ed. John Walsh, Colin Haydon and Stephen Taylor (Cambridge: Cambridge University Press, 1993). For beauty of writing and catholicity of spirit, Gordon Rupp's final book, *Religion in England, 1688–1791* (Oxford: Clarendon Press, 1986) is unlikely ever to be surpassed.

On Dissenters and Roman Catholics in this period, two key works are respectively M. Watts, *The Dissenters, from the Reformation to the French Revolution* (Oxford: Clarendon Press, 1978) and J. Bossy, *The English Catholic Community, 1570–1850* (London: Darton, Longman & Todd, 1975). Important modern studies of the Evangelical Revival include *A History of the Methodist Church in Great Britain*, ed. R. Davies, A. Raymond George and E. G. Rupp (London: Epworth Press, 1965, 1970 and 1980); D. W. Bebbington, *Evangelicalism in Modern Britain: A History from the 1730s to the 1980s* (London: Unwin Hyman, 1989); H. Rack, *Reasonable Enthusiast: John Wesley and the Rise of Methodism* (London: Epworth Press, 1989); and W. R. Ward, *The Protestant Evangelical Awakening* (Cambridge: Cambridge University Press, 1992).

The number of books written about Lady Huntingdon herself is growing, although it is still only a tiny fraction of the number written about John Wesley. The first appeared in 1839, nearly 50 years after her death. It is a massive two-volume work called *The Life and Times of the Countess of Huntingdon*. It was published anonymously, but is known to be by A. C. Hobart Seymour. It contains a large amount of information, including extracts from many original documents that have not otherwise survived. There are several problems with Seymour. One is that he has little idea of how to structure a narrative, so that different episodes are jumbled together in a way that makes it difficult to follow. Another is that he is largely uncritical in his approach to Lady Huntingdon and her activities. The most serious criticism of Seymour, however, is that he produces many anecdotes and assertions that are either at odds with known facts, or for which no independent evidence exists. Where he does use documents that have survived, his quotations from them are not always accurate. For all these reasons, he needs to be read with great care.

After Seymour, a number of writers attempted a simplified version of the story he told. These are easier to read, but in other respects must be approached with the same caution as Seymour himself.

From the middle of the twentieth century there has been renewed academic interest in Lady Huntingdon. This attention – which took the form both of research theses and books – was prompted in part by the Cheshunt archive, mentioned below, which became generally available to researchers from the 1960s. Edwin Welch, the archivist who classified the Cheshunt papers, published *Spiritual Pilgrim: A Reassessment of the Life of the Countess of Huntingdon* in 1995 (Cardiff: University of Wales Press). It is an invaluable tool in unpicking the complex story of Lady Huntingdon's family background, as well as her life and work. This was followed by Boyd Stanley Schlenther, *Queen of the Methodists: The Countess of Huntingdon and the Eighteenth*

Century Crisis of Faith and Society (Bishop Auckland: Durham Academic Press, 1997). This is a scholarly and highly enjoyable account of Lady Huntingdon's career, although I have not always agreed with the dramatic interpretation that Dr Schlenther places on some of the sources. Nor do I share his view that Lady Huntingdon's high-flown evangelical language provides much actual insight into her character and motivation. Faith Cook's *Selina, Countess of Huntingdon: Her Pivotal Role in the 18th Century Evangelical Awakening* (Edinburgh and Carlisle, PA: Banner of Truth Trust, 2001) is written from a position of stated sympathy with Lady Huntingdon's beliefs and objectives; she makes high claims for the impact that Lady Huntingdon had upon eighteenth-century society, but is nevertheless frank about her subject's failings. Finally, my own *The Countess of Huntingdon's Connexion: A Sect in Action in Eighteenth Century England* (Oxford: Oxford University Press, 2003) focused on the operation of the Connexion itself, rather than its founder, using the material to show how a revivalist group functioned in the later eighteenth century.

Many letters to and from Lady Huntingdon have survived. Some are to be found among her family papers, which are split between Leicester and California; others are in the Methodist archives in Manchester; a good number are scattered in university libraries around the world. The most significant single collection, as indicated above, is that belonging to the Cheshunt Foundation, which traces its origins back to Lady Huntingdon's college at Trevecca, and which is now housed at Westminster College, Cambridge. A list of all the main manuscript holdings is at the end of this note. Only a few of the letters that Lady Huntingdon wrote or received have so far appeared in print.

The present book is based extensively on original documents. Sources for the highlighted quotations are included with them. Those readers wishing to identify the source of other statements made in this book will in most cases find them in the footnotes to my earlier book on the Connexion, or in the foot- or endnotes of the books by Welch and Schlenther mentioned above. I am happy to deal with other queries on source material put to me through the publishers.

Principal Manuscript Sources

Bridwell Library, Southern Methodist University, Dallas: letters of Lady Huntingdon

Cheshunt College Foundation, Westminster College, Cambridge: archives of the Countess of Huntingdon's Connexion and College

Congregational Library, Dr Williams's Library, London: Sir John Bickerton Williams Collection (letters of Lady Huntingdon and others)

Countess of Huntingdon Connexion Archives, Rayleigh: letters of Lady Huntingdon and others

Drew University Library, Madison, New Jersey: letters to and from Lady Huntingdon

Emory University Library, Atlanta: correspondence of Lady Huntingdon

Gloucester Record Office: Ebley Chapel Records (letters to Lady Huntingdon and others)

Huntington Library, San Marino, California: Hastings family papers

John Rylands Library, Manchester: letters of Lady Huntingdon

Leicester Record Office: Hastings family papers

Methodist Connexional Archives, John Rylands Library, Manchester: letters of Lady Huntingdon, Fletcher and Ingham; letters to Charles Wesley

National Library of Wales: the Trevecka Letters; the Diary of Howell Harris; letters to Lady Huntingdon

Index

Addington, Dr 188
Aldridge, William 98
Aldwinkle,
    Northamptonshire 74–6,
    88
American War of
    Independence 157
antinomianism 24, 139, 146,
    195
Apostolic Society 193–4, 201
Arminianism 23, 132, 143
Articles of Faith (of the
    Connexion) 184
Ashby-de-la-Zouch 40, 41, 56

'bands' in Wesleyan
    Methodism 117
Baptists 1
Barlow, Ann 57
Barnard, Thomas 31–2
Bath 26, 28, 70–2, 78, 86, 97,
    159, 177, 186, 195, 199
    Sunday school 125
Bedford 54
Bell, George 82

Bencoolen 149, 150, 172
Benezet, Anthony 148
Benson, Joseph 133, 136, 165
Berkhamstead 188
Berkshire 76
Berridge, John 60, 83, 84,
    90–1, 140, 186
Best, George 109, 126, 189,
    193
Bethesda Orphan
    House 147ff, 172, 190
Birmingham 126
Boehme, Jacob 41
Bold, John 8
Bolingbroke, Lord 40, 43
Book of Common Prayer
    16–17, 18, 108, 124
    used in the Connexion 120–1
Bradford, John 194, 195
Bray, Thomas 6
Brecon 96
Bridgewater 97, 105, 111
Brighton 65–6, 69, 70, 72, 74,
    79, 84, 98, 111, 118–19, 124,
    177

Bristol 85, 104, 128, 195
Brussels 190–1
Burnett, George 88

Calvinism 23–4, 58, 87–8,
   132, 143, 146, 184, 194
Cambridge 77, 89, 90, 173,
   182
chapel committees 115–6, 126
Charles, Thomas 200
Cheshunt College,
   Cambridge 202
Cheshunt College,
   Hertfordshire 201, 202
Chesterfield, Lord 27, 43,
   52–3, 64, 66
Chichester 116, 118
children's work 124–5
Church of England
 in the 17th and 18th
   centuries 3–6
 Holy Communion, frequency
   of 5–6, 120
 pluralism and non-residence
   in 4–5
 High Church traditions
   13–14, 18
 evangelicals in 21–2
 clergy attitudes to the
   Connexion 100, 102–3,
   121–2
 catechism 124
Clifton, Bristol 56
Clapham Sect 60

Clark, Samuel 105
Clarke, Samuel 11
clerical dress 121–2
Cook, Joseph 152
Coram, Thomas 7, 30
Corfe Castle 121
Cornwall 142, 198
Cosson, John 152, 153, 156
Countess of Huntingdon's
   Connexion x
Crole, Anthony 121–2

Dartmouth, Lord 84
Davies, Howel 19
De Courcy, Richard 78
deism 10
Denham (? Edmund) 111
Devon 104, 110, 113, 183,
   186
Dewsbury, Yorkshire 80
Derbyshire 30, 72, 104
Dissenters 2, 11–12, 22–3, 90,
   91, 123, 179
 attitudes to the
   Connexion 97, 102, 104
Dixon, Dr George 87
Doddridge, Dr Philip 22,
   42–3, 50–1, 57, 77, 188
 academy at Northampton 91
Donnington Park,
   Leicestershire 25, 55
Douglass, Lord 190
Drummond, Robert,
   Archbishop of York 4–5

East Anglia 108, 198

East Indies 149

Easterbrook, Joseph 93

Eccles, Charles Stuart 151

Edwin, Catherine 57

Elland Clerical Society 88–9

Ellis, William 165

Erskine, Lady Anne 109, 188–9, 196

resists the Plan of Association 199–200

Evangelical Revival 16ff

Everton, Bedfordshire 60

Exeter, Bishop of 49

Feathers Tavern petition 11

Ferrers, 2nd Earl (Lady Huntingdon's father) 25

Ferrers, 4th Earl 61–2, 73

Fletcher, John 60, 79, 88

as president of Trevecca college 91, 93–4, 164–5

resigns 136, 146

role in the 1770s controversy 138–9, 141

French Revolution 191–2

George II 30

Georgia 147–8, 157

proposed University of 161–2

Glascott, Craddock 76, 104–5, 109, 112–13, 158, 175, 180, 186

considers secession 181, 182, 183

Glazebrook, James 94, 97–8, 100, 110

ordained in the Church of England 172–3

Glenorchy, Viscountess 145, 202

Glorious Revolution of 1688 2, 67, 176

Gloucester 111, 125

Gospel Magazine 137

Grimsby 142

Grinfield, Ann 56–57, 63

Habersham, James 147

Harris, Howel 19–20, 42, 69, 73, 84

begins preaching for Lady Huntingdon 38, 40–41

relations with Wesleys and Whitefield 45–7

retreats to Wales 46

re-emerges 58

attitude to women preaching 78

as ecumenist 82, 85, 86

and Trevecca college 91–2

Hartley, Thomas 56

Hastings, Lady Anne 58

Hastings, Lady Betty 25–6, 31, 32, 33, 66

Hastings, Elizabeth (Lady Huntingdon's daughter)

– *see Moira, Elizabeth, Countess of*

Hastings, Lady Frances 25, 50

Hastings, Francis, 10th Earl of Huntingdon 27, 40, 52–3, 54

Hastings, Henry (Lady Huntingdon's son) 40, 61, 65

Hastings, Lady Margaret – *see Ingham, Lady Margaret*

Hastings, Selina, Countess of Huntingdon:

early life 25

marriage 25

homes 27

interest in politics 28–30

conversion 31ff

early influence on the revival 34, 45

moves towards Calvinism 36

widowed 40

interest in mysticism 41–42

ministry to the upper classes 43–4

relations with her children 53–5, 61, 83–4

moves to Clifton 56–58

relations with John Wesley 56, 83–6, 133–4

invasion fears in 1759 63

begins work in Brighton 65–6

evangelism in Sussex 68–70

opens Bath chapel 70–2

collects clergy 73–8

and the Aldwinkle affair 75–6

attitude to women preaching 78–9

attitudes to Moravians in the 1760s 81–2

founds Trevecca college 90–6

encourages itinerant preaching 96ff

limited financial resources 106–7

control of preachers and congregations 110–12, 115–16, 126–30

as hymn-writer 122–3

attitude to children's work 124–5

and the financing of the Connexion 125–9

reaction to Wesley's Conference Minutes of 1770 135ff

rivalry with the Wesleyans 142–3

suspicion of the Tabernacle Connexion 144–5

likewise of Rowland Hill and Lady Glenorchy 145

inherits Bethesda Orphan House 147ff

relationship with students 154–5, 168–9

plans mission to American
Indians 160–1, 162
considers Connexion
ordination 175
takes over Spa Fields
chapel 179–80
decides on secession 180–4
plans successor to
Trevecca 189–90
European ventures 190–92
dismisses Wills, Taylor, and
Bradford 194–5
plans the continuation of the
Connexion 195ff
death 200
legacy 201ff
Hastings, Selina (Lady
Huntingdon's daughter) 40,
61, 83–4
Hastings, Theophilus, 9th Earl
of Huntingdon 25, 26, 32,
38, 40
Haverfordwest,
Pembrokeshire 144
Haweis, Thomas 73–6, 77, 78,
83, 88, 198, 200, 201
at Spa Fields 180, 181, 182
plans Tahiti expedition 163
resists the Plan of
Association 199
Hawksworth, John 147
Heckmondwike academy 91
Hereford 166
Herefordshire 97

Herrenhaag orphanage 33
Herrnhut, Saxony 18
Hervey, James 58–9
Higson, John 87
Hill, Sir Richard 76, 134, 137,
139, 140
Hill, Rowland 76–7, 140, 141,
143–5
Holmes, John 105
Holy Communion in the
Connexion 69, 116, 119–
120, 151
Hotham, Sir Charles 69
Hotham, Lady Gertrude 66
Huddersfield 60
humanitarian initiatives 7
Hughes, Betty 151, 152, 153,
165
Hutton, James 33
Hull, Christopher 165
hymns 122–4

imputed righteousness 59
Ingham, Benjamin 21, 31, 33,
58
Ingham, Lady Margaret 25,
31, 33, 58
Ireland, James 137
itinerancy 112, 188

Jacobites 29, 36
Jesse, William 78
Johnson, John 162
Johnson, Dr Samuel 9, 95

Jones, Griffiths 19
Jones, Herbert 178, 179
Jones, Theophilus 111

Keen, Robert 143, 159
Kent 72, 198
Kilmorey, Viscountess Mary
  (Lady Huntingdon's
  sister) 32
Kimpton, John 74–5
Kingswood school 93

Lancashire 108
latitudinarianism 12–13, 17
Laurens, Henry 161
Law, William 14, 33, 37,
  41–42
Leighton, Mrs H 82, 92
Lincolnshire 104, 108
Lindsey, Theophilus 11
Lloyd, John 79–80, 200
London, Bishop of 150, 179
London:
  Chelsea 27, 48, 50, 56
  Clapham 60
  Clerkenwell 177, 178
  Downing Street 27
  Enfield Chase 27, 34
  Fetter Lane society 34
  Foundry chapel 34, 82–3
  Hoxton Academy 123
  Lock Hospital 59, 74, 150
  Moorfields Tabernacle 20,
    36, 55, 78, 144, 152

Northampton chapel – see
  Spa Fields
Pantheon, The – see Spa
  Fields
Rotherhithe 107–8
St Anne's, Blackfriars 59
St George's, Hanover
  Square 59
Savile Row 27
Spa Fields chapel 125, 129,
  130, 177ff, 194, 195
Tottenham Court Road
  chapel 20, 55, 152
Wapping 177
West Street chapel 36
Woolwich 151, 158
Long-town, Herefordshire 97
love-feasts 118–19

Madan, Martin 59, 66, 72,
  74–5, 77, 83, 84, 139
Madeley, Shropshire 60, 79,
  93
Margate, David 156–7
Maxfield, Thomas 36, 82–3
McAll, Robert 110–11
Mead, Henry 97–8, 100
Melbourne, Derbyshire
'Methodism' 19, 45
Moira, Elizabeth, Countess
  of 26, 53–4
Moira, Lord – see Rawdon,
  Lord (Lady Huntingdon's
  son-in-law)

Molland, Thomas 120
Moravian Brethren 18–19, 33, 34, 39, 41, 58
in Bedford 54, 81
in Bristol 57–58
at Fulneck 81
in Bath 81–2
Lady Huntingdon's attitude towards 81–2, 92–3
love-feasts revived by 119
More, Hannah 5
Morpeth, Northumberland 198

Necker, Jacques 192
Nelson, John 60
New Brunswick 163
Newton, John 88, 117, 124
Non-jurors 3
Nova Scotia 163

Oat Hall – see Ote Hall
Okely, Francis 92–3
Olivers, Thomas 139, 140
Olney, Buckinghamshire 117, 124
ordination in the Connexion 113, 175–6, 185, 187
Orphan House, Georgia – see Bethesda
Ostend 190, 191
Ote Hall 68–9, 72
Oxford 20–1, 74, 76, 78, 90, 173
'Holy Club' 20–21, 124
St Edmund Hall case 87–8, 94, 134

Peckwell, Henry 106, 181
Pentycross, Thomas 181
Perfection, doctrine of 24, 35, 83
Pewsey, Wiltshire 78
Phillips, David 162
Phillips, Samuel 166
Pierce, Samuel Eyles 169
Piercy, Richard 151, 153
Piercy, William 150–1, 153–60, 174
refuses to secede from the Church of England 158
Plan of Association 197–200
Powley, Matthew 79–80
Powys, Thomas 137
preaching rounds 105–6, 109, 110
predestination 23, 34–5, 58, 131–2, 173
Presbyterians 1, 69
Pritchard, David 116
Putcham, near Bridgewater 110–11

Quakers and Quakerism 41, 78

Raikes, Raymond 125

Rawdon, Lord (Lady Huntingdon's son-in-law) 53, 54
Rawdon, Lord (Lady Huntingdon's grandson) 54
Reformation, The 1, 3, 16
religious societies 7, 117
Restoration of Charles II in 1660 1, 2
Rodborough Connexion 143–4
Roman Catholics 2–3
  Lady Huntingdon's attitude towards 161–2, 190, 192
Romaine, William 59, 69, 72, 83, 84, 186
Ross-on-Wye 97, 100
Rowlands, Daniel 19
Rowlands, Nathaniel 195

St Ives, Cornwall 37
salvation 23–4
Savannah, Georgia 147
scientific developments 9–10
Seager, S. 126
Selina (Bethesda slave) 149
Sellon, William 178–9, 180, 186
Shepherd, Edward 80
Shirley, Mary, Countess Ferrers (Lady Huntingdon's mother) 25
Shirley, Walter 73, 76, 77, 78. 119, 124, 144

opposes Wesley's Minutes 137–8
Shropshire 78
Skrine, Elizabeth 57
sin 16–17, 131
Slaithwaite, Yorkshire 80
slavery, attitudes towards 148–9, 155, 156
'societies' in Connexion congregations 117–18
Society for Propagating the Gospel (SPG) 6, 150
Society for Promoting Christian Knowledge (SPCK) 6, 30, 89
South Carolina 156, 157, 160
South Petherton, Somerset 105
Stillingfleet, James 88
'stillness' 34, 41
Stonehouse, George 63
Sunday schools 125
Sussex 68–70, 78
Suter, Thomas 167
Swansea 111
Swedenborg, Emanuel 56

Tabernacle Connexion 20, 108, 143–5, 151, 159
Tahiti 163
Taylor, Bishop Jeremy 14, 33
Taylor, William 109, 178, 179, 181, 184, 185, 194, 195

Thirty-nine Articles 17–18, 164, 184

Toleration Act of 1689 3, 67–8, 69, 176

Toplady, Augustus 66, 134

Torbay, Devon 104

Townsend, Joseph 77

Townsend, Judith 77

Travelling Fund 129

Trevecca College 60, 189
  opening 91ff
  students engage in itinerant preaching 96–9, 126, 167, 193
  influence on Dissenters 123
  funding of students 126–7
  impact of the 1770 controversy upon 136, 141, 146
  inauguration of the Bethesda mission 151–2
  academic standards 164, 166–7
  teaching at 165–6
  legacy of 170
  students ordained into the Church of England 172–4
  or by the Dissenters 174
  planning for successor institution 189–90, 192–4, 201

Trevecka settlement 39, 91, 92

Trinity, doctrine of 11

Tunbridge Wells 72, 177

Venn, Henry 59, 72, 73, 84, 186

Venn, John 60

violence against evangelical preachers 103

Wales, Frederick, Prince of 30, 44, 63

Wales 198
  revival in 19–20

Wallingford, Oxfordshire 111

Walpole, Horace 55, 71

Wase, Benjamin 169

Washington, George 160–1

Watson, Bishop Richard 11

Watts, Isaac 123

Welsh Association 19

Welsh clergy 109, 182, 198, 200

Wesley, Charles 20, 21, 34, 35, 91
  and Lady Huntingdon 36, 51–2, 56, 84–6
  assists at the Bath chapel 80
  attitude to the controversy of 1770 137, 140–1

Wesley, John 20
  and the Moravians 18–19, 34
  conversion 21
  early contacts with Lady Huntingdon 34, 35
  relations with Harris and Whitefield 45, 133
  friction with Lady Huntingdon 56, 83–4

impressed by Berridge 60
and the Toleration Act 67–8,
    176–7
attitude to women
    preaching 78
Bell/Maxfield affair 82–3
training for lay preachers 91
attitude to Trevecca
    college 95–6
and the Conference Minutes
    of 1770 134–5
attitude to slavery 148
Wesley, Sarah (wife of
    Charles) 51, 52
West, Daniel 143
Weymouth 105
White, William 105
Whitefield, George 20, 26, 35,
    51, 56, 66, 73, 77, 106, 128
appointed chaplain to Lady
    Huntingdon 43
flatters her 44
relations with the
    Wesleys 45, 83, 84, 85–6
opens Tunbridge Wells
    chapel 72
opens Trevecca College 96
last contacts with John
    Wesley 133
death 133, 136, 143, 147
and the Bethesda Orphan
    House 147–8

and slavery 148
Williams, John (first master at
    Trevecca) 93
Williams, John (last master at
    Trevecca) 166
Williams, William (of
    Pantecelyn) 166
Williams (student) 111
Wills, Thomas 108, 109, 126,
    158, 181, 196, 197, 201
secedes from the Church of
    England 183–4
performs first Connexion
    ordination 185
and the Brussels
    mission 190–1
dismissed from the
    Connexion 193–5
pays tribute to Lady
    Huntingdon 203
Wills, Mrs Selina 180
Wivelsfield, Sussex 68, 69
The Whole Duty of Man 14
women preachers 78–9
Woodforde, James 7–8, 74
Woolston, Thomas 10

Yelling, Cambridgeshire 60
Yorkshire 78, 104, 108

Zinzendorff, Count
    Nicholas 18